AUTISM HEALED

ONE WOMAN'S FIGHT TO SAVE HER SONS

Deborah M. A. McDermott

ISBN: 978-1-7951-1123-2
Copyright © 2019 Deborah M. A. McDermott
Website: deborahmamcdermott.com

FOREWORD

I was privileged to be the one who prayed for Timothy and James McDermott to be healed of Asperger's Syndrome and autism, but the more I've learned about their miraculous healings, the more I've realized it was Deborah's tenacious faith that produced this miracle.

We can only imagine what Deborah and her husband, Christopher, went through all those years of seeing their beloved children tormented day and night. Very few people and very few marriages could have survived such trauma. In this book, Deborah does an excellent job of baring her soul to describe what her experience was like. You will feel what she felt.

Those of you who have found yourself in nearly unbearable circumstances will immediately identify with the heartaches and challenges that Deborah so clearly presents. But it won't stop there. She will show you how the Lord encouraged her and brought her through when she literally had no one else to turn to.

You will also discover that her boys' healing wasn't instantaneous. It was a process, and during that process, her faith was tested and even faltered at times. But God's grace and mercy were constant, as He kept encouraging her. Deborah's testimony will encourage you to stand, regardless of your circumstances.

You will also learn what I consider to be a key component of this story: Deborah refused to make peace with what was destroying her children. There was pressure from every side to accept this as God's will or just as a matter of fact, but Deborah had a word from God that made all the difference. Her resistance was critical.

This story is a modern-day example of how nothing is impossible to those who believe. Many read stories of miracles in the Bible but wonder if such miracles can happen today. This testimony proves that it can and does. The McDermotts have doctors' reports to verify it. It happened for Deborah and her boys, and it can happen for you.

After his healing, Timothy came to the United States and lived on his own for three years while attending Charis Bible College. He has been a star in many of our musicals and was consistently one of the most popular students in the college. Everyone loves Timothy! James has also proven the healing power of God in his life, and we are all excited to see what the Lord has planned for him as he grows up and embarks on his future.

This book is a faith builder. If you will open your heart and receive the lessons taught within these pages, the Lord will do for you what He has done for the McDermotts. God loves you and those you are praying for more than you do. He wants you well. I pray that the seeds of truth sown through this book will sprout and grow into your full-grown miracle.

Andrew Wommack
President and Founder,
Andrew Wommack Ministries and Charis Bible College

ACKNOWLEDGEMENTS

Thank you Timothy and James for allowing me to share your stories, for your input, feedback, and reminding me to laugh! You are a constant reminder of the goodness of God, and I love you so much.

Thank you to all the ministries who taught me the true gospel, revealed God to me, and fed my hope and faith. Joyce Meyer, Kenneth and Gloria Copeland, Creflo Dollar, Joel Osteen and Andrew Wommack Ministries.

"How beautiful are the feet of those who preach the gospel of peace. Who bring glad tidings of good things." Romans 10:15.

Stephen Bransford, thanks for all your support, input, encouragement and friendship. What a blessing.

Andrew and Jamie Wommack, thank you from the bottom of my heart. Words cannot adequately express my love and gratitude to you. Your untiring commitment to reveal the true nature of God through your ministry and Charis Bible College, has changed our lives.

And finally, to my husband, Christopher, thanks for your ruthless editing, and taking time out of your crazy schedule to help me sort this book out. Your love, patience, support, and encouragement through it all means everything to me.

Deborah McDermott
February 2019

INTRODUCTION

I can still hear her voice, so crisp and businesslike: "Mrs. McDermott, your son has autism. In fact, he has a form called Asperger's Syndrome."

She spoke with authority, as if she knew everything and I knew absolutely nothing. After all, she was the esteemed therapist, and I was merely a physically and emotionally wrecked mother; my thoughts and opinions hardly worthy of consideration.

"You need to make friends with it, Mrs. McDermott." She paused, scrutinizing me, while I grit my teeth and stared, unseeing out of the window. "I'm very serious. You must face facts and make friends with the diagnosis."

Make friends with it?

It?

But this "it" I'm supposed to make friends with—what is it? It's something invisible attached to my son. It makes his life such hell, yet he looks normal. You can't see this "it," but it manifests in his life like a many-tentacled octopus. Malignant tentacles reaching into his brain, his gut, his joints, his senses, his emotions.

My boy can see the world outside but can't engage with it. Can't connect with it, be a part of it. He longs to join the people who live life around him—to interact with them, to have friends—but the steel bars of autism shut him in.

He's locked in a kind of invisible prison as the octopus tentacles do their work—the crippling anxiety rendering him mute, the brain taking so long—too long—to process the garbled sounds he hears, turning them into words he can understand. Confusion. Lights too bright, sounds too loud, smells too strong, colors too dazzling. Everything is too much, too much, too much!

Oh yes, the prison bars are doing their job just fine as the malignant, writhing octopus wraps another tentacle around its prisoner. I can see it nodding in smug agreement with the therapist. *Yes*, it whispers with a wink, *that's right, just make friends with me.*

"Mrs. McDermott, as a professional who deals with autism, I perfectly understand why you might be in denial. But I'm telling you, it's time to accept his disability; accept that it's a part of who he is. And, of course, you must accept that there is no cure."

A knife to my heart! No hope! No cure! No way to break these bars and let my son out. No way to kill the octopus and rip those evil tentacles out of his body and mind. No way to set him free. No cure… no hope….

I look at him, my lovely son, his straight brown hair falling across his forehead. His beautiful green eyes, so bright, so trusting, so hopeful… but no, not hopeful now. Not anymore. Those once bright eyes are becoming duller, sadder.

There is a shadow deepening in the cage he inhabits. The octopus is growing larger, taking strength from my beautiful boy, who is disappearing behind the bars of steel and the squirming tentacles that have wrapped around him, slowly sucking the spirit and the life from him, pulling him further and further away.

I want to scream, to reach into the cage and pull him out, to drag him to safety, but I can't, I can't. I can't help him.

"Mrs. McDermott, please understand, your son is depressed. We believe the extreme mood swings are signs of bipolar disorder. He is at risk of suicide, and we must get him on stabilizing medication as soon as possible."

All the voices of all the therapists and experts are now shouting at me, surrounding me with their words. Just words, words... but no solutions.

Not to mention the clinical reports I have been forced to read, one upon another: speech and language, occupational therapy, educational psychology, nutritional therapy, neuropsychology. Each category adding strange new words to the cacophony—dysexecutive syndrome, hyperlexia, dyspraxia, learning difficulties, ADHD, sleeping disorders, brain damage, leaky gut syndrome, selective mutism, dyscalculia, Asperger's Syndrome, autism, depression, and now—*suicide!?*

In my mind, the words shout and shout and shout at me: *There is no cure, but we can manage the symptoms, medicate the symptoms. You'll learn coping strategies, Mrs. McDermott, behavior modification. Yes, we can help to modify, manage, medicate, cope. You will survive, you will manage, but you will need to medicate.*

My lovely, lovely boy, slipping from my grasp into the clutches of the enemy. But don't worry son, we'll medicate you, so it will be OK. You'll be locked in that prison forever, but you'll be happy in your own way. Drugged so that we might make it through the day, the week, the year... the lifetime.

Dear God! The unutterable, hopeless despair of it all.

It's 2 a.m., and I have not slept. The words are torturing me still. I see the therapist's disapproving scowl, as she says, "This is not about you, Mrs. McDermott. Pull yourself together. You need to accept the diagnosis, and yes, make friends with it. After all," she states matter-of-factly, "it is simply who he is."

Who he is? That is who my boy is? I must get over it? Deal with it? Accept it? *MAKE FRIENDS WITH IT?*

Suddenly the pain gives way to a rage and a fury. I lie there, fists clenched, my body drenched in sweat, and I scream in my mind, "Never! Never! *NEVER!*"

I know the truth. I will never make friends with it. AUTISM IS THE ENEMY!

How many times have I heard the prevailing wisdom: "If you reject the autism, you reject the child. Because, after all, autism is just a bunch of issues that are part of his make-up.

"And if you hate and reject the autistic characteristics, you are hating and rejecting the child"?

"Come on, Mrs. McDermott, your son's autism runs through every cell of his body. Wanting to get rid of it means you want to get rid of him. You don't want that, do you?"

Will we really do anything to make our child better? Will we?

The therapist is not my friend. She is my highly paid counselor. Realizing how desperate I am, she asks in a tone of professional sympathy, "Do you have someone in your life who loves you completely and unconditionally? Who really knows you and understands you? Someone who genuinely hears you and cares about your life? With whom you can be transparent and real, without criticism, without gossiping behind your back or betraying your vulnerability? A parent or grandparent? An aunty or family friend?"

The answer is yes, but I will not answer aloud. She does not deserve to know about Mary.

Mary is wonderful. She loves me, adores me. I can do no wrong with Mary. I can open my heart and soul to her. She is infinitely interested in all the minutiae of my life.

She knows my past and is deeply concerned about my future. She adores my sons and my husband. She feels my pain. She laughs with me and cries with me. I'm safe with Mary.

Mary is my diary. I'm glad she's here because I have a beautiful story to tell her now. A story that bares my soul and at times is almost impossible to write, but a story that is impossible not to write. A story of tragedy turned to triumph.

You see, I have made my choice. I *will* do anything to heal my children. *Anything!*

So, I am turning to Mary now, reaching for my pen so that I can share the burden of my story with her. So that she can know the lows I have sunk to, the heights I have climbed, and the vistas I have seen.

Because there is only one question that I want Mary to answer. And that I want you to answer before you read further:

Do you believe in miracles?

CHAPTER 1

Dear Mary,

Well Mary, I married him. Yes, just like Jane Eyre herself, I married my gorgeous Englishman—6 feet 2 inches tall, dark mane of hair, with a sweet-sardonic smile that says, *I bequeath thee my kingdom*. I'm so happy, even though I really do miss South Africa sometimes.

It's 1995, and two years since I left my home. I spent my whole life there, but then it changed. It wasn't safe anymore, so I packed everything up, and on a wing and a prayer, arrived at Heathrow very late one night in March and talked my way into the UK. It was touch-and-go whether they would send me back. But as you already know, Mary, I have angels by my side, and through the grace of God they let me stay (but on the condition that I did not exceed my six-month tourist visa).

So, five months and three weeks later, I married the man of my dreams then spent the next week convincing the authorities that it wasn't a marriage of convenience. You knew it wasn't, Mary, and when they saw our wedding pictures and our honeymoon snaps from Scotland, they were convinced as well.

So, after all that, I'm now ready to have my little English family.

My husband, Christopher, whom I met quite by chance in a shopping center back in Johannesburg, is a goldsmith. An honest, if not particularly well-paying job, but it will be enough I'm sure. We'll make a life for ourselves in this grey, northern island, and I'll put to memory the stark, piercing light of the Highveld and the great rolling hills of Natal.

And, I must try to lose my accent if I can. I've been told that you can spend a lot of time in the UK, not being from the UK.

But I'm so broody, Mary! Christopher says he can hear my body clock ticking like Big Ben.

Bong! Imagine, a new little life inside of me...

Bong! A new little family...

Bong! ...here, in our little part of England.

Oh Mary, I ache with longing and hope. I have such dreams for us and for our children.

CHAPTER 2

Dear Mary,

It's happened! I've wasted so many of these test kits, but finally I have one that is positive.

There's a little blue line that says: "Hey you, there, the one who just peed on this stick. Yes you. Guess what? You're pregnant!"

Christopher keeps hugging me and laughing, "I'm going to be a dad… Ah, my darling, I can't believe it. We're going to have a little McDermott."

Dear Mary,

When we found out that news a couple of months ago, things had been OK. We were still renting, granted, but we were sure that in time we could save up to get a deposit to buy a house. We both had decent jobs working in the family jewelry business. We were settled and happy. The perfect time to start a family.

But just a few weeks later the company went out of business (and I am too tired to go into the details, but suffice to say, it seemed like one missed opportunity after another), and now we are both unemployed and not far from being broke.

But Christopher has found a goldsmith's position in another town. "Don't worry, my darling," Christopher says. "We'll move, and start again; it'll be OK, you gorgeous big 'heffalump' you."

He laughed, kissing my belly gently. "In fact, let's jump in the car right now, drive over, and have a look around to see if we can find a place to live."

Dear Mary,
　Have you seen the little country lanes in England? Of course you have. You are by my side always, so you already know that they are charming and beautiful. Lush and green in the summer (a green so green that I never saw in South Africa, probably because of all the rain they have here). But also, really narrow, with thick, knotted hedges on either side.
　Well, we were traveling down such a lane, enjoying the beautiful late summer countryside, when a huge truck topped the ridge ahead, approaching on our side of the road.
　There was no time to think or act really. I just braced myself as the driver hit his brakes so hard that great clouds of white smoke poured from underneath the truck, a great squalling sound reverberated through our car, and all I could smell was burning rubber.
　He was going too fast to stop. Christopher slammed on the breaks and swerved into the hedge. The truck roared past, missing us by an inch.
　Sometimes I wonder about the driver of that truck. I suppose he can't know the chain of events he unleashed that bright summer's day in 1995. Did he check his rearview mirrors to see that we had survived without hitting anything substantial, and then take the next bend in the road (albeit a bit slower now and on the right side), and then not give us any more thought? A moment passed, lives intersecting for a brief dramatic second before splintering off again; but this time in different and difficult new directions.
　Because you see, Mary, hours after this near miss, the contractions started. I was only 24 weeks pregnant.

CHAPTER 3

Dear Mary,

Here I am now in Shrewsbury Hospital, watching my contractions register on a screen by my bed. I feel so helpless. But you know this. Even though I trained as a nurse, hospitals seem to me almost designed by default to disempower you.

They are giving me Retardin via a drip, but the contractions keep coming in waves. A nurse came in just now to check the readouts from the machine measuring the contractions. She patted my hand gently and whispered, "I'm so sorry my dear," and then immediately left the room and returned a few minutes later with a woman who introduced herself as the hospital's grief counselor.

"It looks very much like the baby is coming soon," she said. "You need to understand that the chance of a 24-week baby surviving is less than 50%, and we have no beds left in our neonatal intensive care. There is an ambulance on standby to take the baby to another hospital."

I'm quite terrified. "Can't you take me to that hospital now?" I asked, agonized about the prospect of my tiny baby being whisked away, only to die in an ambulance.

"I'm sorry, we just can't risk it," my doctor explained. "Every time you move, the contractions speed up. Transporting you to another hospital might prompt the baby to come now. The best I can do is promise to have an ambulance on standby to transport your baby as soon as possible. But only after it is born!"

My heart is thumping away as though I've been doing an hour of aerobics. Apparently, it's the medication. It's hard to be calm with these contractions going on and on. My pulse is racing like a train hurtling through an endless dark tunnel, with no pinprick of light in the distance to save me.

I've been praying, Mary, begging God, to please not take my baby, to please save this little life.

They have just taken the IV out and are stopping the Retardin. The doctors are worried my heart can't take any more. A minute ago, I sneezed, and immediately the contractions started again.

"Stop being such a traitor," I whispered furiously to my belly. "Stop trying to push out my baby. Just stop it!"

Dear Mary,

You know that we survived, that the contractions did indeed stop. Well, perhaps not stop completely, but enough for my little baby to stay inside. To stay "cooking," as Christopher so delicately put it.

One day at a time, Mary. No, one hour at a time. That's what it's been like. But every minute and every hour eventually turns into another day. And each day is precious. Each day gives my baby a chance to develop and grow, to stay safe until it's ready to join us in our big, bright world.

Christopher's been sitting by my bed, day after day, holding my hand and trying to make me smile. It's been three weeks now, and I'm going home from the hospital today.

This morning the doctor reviewed my records with a deep sigh. "We've done everything we can do," he admitted. "I'm sending you home to rest, and all we can do now is hope for the best." Even modern medicine has its limits, it would seem.

CHAPTER 4

Dear Mary,

Christopher brought me home from the hospital and helped me to bed. While he did this, I spent a lot of time praying. *Stay in, stay in. Lord help me. Keep my little baby safe and in my tummy.*

Over the next few weeks, things did indeed calm down, and the contractions finally stopped. I was so grateful.

I kept thanking God because I felt stronger and healthier with each passing day. So much so that when I reached the seventh month of my pregnancy, we packed up the house and moved to a rental in Leominster, near to where Christopher had found a job.

What strange names some of these English towns have, Mary. For the first few weeks I went around the town calling it "Leo minster," presuming it was called as it was spelled. Only to discover that it's actually pronounced "Lemster." No wonder the locals looked at me in a funny way: "Oh, here comes that South African again who seems to be living in a completely different town than the rest of us."

But what a place to be our lovely baby's first home. Out here in the quiet, lush farmlands of Herefordshire, almost on the border of England and Wales.

The last two months of my pregnancy have gone well, and my water broke the day before my due date.

Like all new responsible parents to be, we'd been to all the antenatal classes, read most of the books (or at least I have—Christopher seemed to lose interest when the pictures got a bit more "graphic"), and we even had a bag packed ready for this very moment.

So, there was no panic as Christopher drove me to the hospital. I had managed to keep my little baby safe, and now, now, Mary, this was the right time for him to be born.

Dear Mary,

Only of course, it wasn't. We arrived at the hospital to discover that although my water had broken, the actual contractions hadn't started. "So, what should we do?" we asked the midwife. "Well," she said, "you'll have to go home and wait for them to start, and then come back in again."

We looked at each other a bit lost because this hadn't been covered in any of the books we'd read. Then she said helpfully, "You could try going for a nice long walk. That might do the trick."

I'm not sure the nature reserve just outside of Leominster had ever seen anything like it. There I was, much to the amusement of the other walkers, leaping up and down, hopping and dancing around in a valiant effort to get the contractions started. Christopher just shrugged at people as they walked past, saying, "She's pregnant," which I think he hoped would explain everything.

After all the time I had spent being still and praying that the contractions would stop while in the hospital, I was now prancing around like a nymph (albeit a heavily pregnant one), trying to convince my baby it was OK to come out into the world. But after three miles of this with no visible signs of success, and now greatly in need of a bath, we went home.

It was the middle of January 1996 and freezing cold (it was the coldest winter in 20 years). And somehow, we'd run out of heating oil, which meant no central heating and no hot water! How had this happened? Well, neither Christopher nor I had never had a property that required heating oil, and because it was so expensive (for our modest budget anyway), we had optimistically assumed we had more than we did. But we didn't. So, I was shivering away like a beached whale in a little puddle of water, while Christopher trooped up and down the stairs with kettles of water heated on a hot plate (thank goodness we still had electricity).

We laughed and laughed, as I tried to splash the water over my huge body. "I can't reach my feet!" I said to Christopher. "In fact, I can't even see my feet! Will you dry them for me?"

I was leaning on his shoulder, laughing, as he feigned subservience, drying my feet and mumbling, "Your wish is my command, my little heffalump." Then my laugh turned into a scream, as my nails bit ungratefully into his shoulder.

Don't rush to the hospital, the books advised. Relax, make some sandwiches; you will have lots of time between contractions. But within a few minutes the next contraction ripped through my body. We weren't laughing now.

No. Now Christopher was speeding towards Hereford Hospital, looking absolutely terrified, while trying to make reassuring noises about "keeping calm."

I was in full-blown labor, and if we weren't careful, I was going to give birth in the car.

Dear Mary,

You know, of all people, that I really wanted an epidural. I had consoled myself about the anticipated pain of childbirth by saying quietly, "Don't worry, Debs, you'll have an epidural, and it will be fine."

However, by the time we arrived at the hospital with my contractions now coming every couple of minutes, it was too late for the epidural I'd hoped for. I was just going to have to do it the traditional way.

And three hours later, filled with awe, wonder, and gratitude, we welcomed Timothy-Julian Christopher Geoffrey McDermott into the world.

Oh Mary, he is so beautiful! A shock of black hair, 8 pounds 9 ounces, and perfect, just perfect. When Christopher held him, tears ran down his cheeks, as he whispered, "My son, my son..." with a look of tender amazement, kissing me, then the baby, and me again.

Later, when the hospital was quiet and everyone else slept, I held baby Timmy and looked at his beautiful face. I felt overwhelmed that the responsibility for this tiny life belonged to Christopher and me.

I whispered to God, "I don't know how to do this. Please help me raise him." Then, I thought about the oath that doctors take: "Father, at the very least, please help me do no harm."

As I stared at his little face, sleeping in my arms, I knew I would fight for him with every breath of my body. I would live, die, or even kill for him.

Goodness, Mary, when this little life was delivered, I felt like a new me was also born at the very same time.

CHAPTER 5

Dear Mary,

Christopher's boss has just been to visit. I was embarrassed about the messy house, but so proud to show off our little four-day-old baby boy.

I had assumed that was why he came over—to see the baby and congratulate us. Christopher, proudly holding his little son, said, "He's called Timothy."

But his boss looked at the baby in a vague, distracted way, and said, "Actually Chris, he isn't really the reason I have come to see you. There are issues at work, and I'm afraid I'm going to have to lay you off. You needn't come back in next week." And before we had time to say anything, he had left.

Christopher and I stared at one another in open-mouthed shock. We didn't see that coming. We moved to "Lemster" especially for his work and had only been here a few months.

Now what do we do? Christopher's face went as white as a sheet as he passed the now-screaming baby to me, and then silently left the room.

Dear Mary,

These past three months have been an absolute blur. Oh, my goodness, this is harrowing, but I will tell it like it is. I am always frank with you, Mary. Timothy just cries and cries! I know something's wrong, even though the midwife thinks it's only colic. The medication doesn't help. And when I finally get him to sleep, the smallest disturbance wakes him, his little face puckers up and turns red, and he starts crying again. He gets an hour's sleep here, and maybe 90 minutes there. But he's feeding well; he's a ravenous little fellow. So that's something.

The days are going by in a confusion of feeds, nappy changes, endless pacing and soothing, with moments of snatched unconsciousness (which you can't call sleep because it's never long enough).

Timothy still doesn't seem to know the difference between night and day. The doctor has prescribed infant pain medication, which helps a bit. But he won't lie flat and will only sleep upright in our arms. This is something that is both very special and very torturous because the nights are so very, very long.

Christopher opened up a bit yesterday about the day he was laid off. He looked really sheepish about the whole thing, before blurting out, "To be honest, Deb, I have never been so relieved in my life; I hated that job! In fact, I hate working in jewelry. I'm sorry, love, but after I got over the shock, I was secretly delighted. I never want to work in that industry again. I'm going to do something else. I don't know what yet, but I am determined to try something new."

With a wife and baby to support, he couldn't have justified leaving the job. But now this is an opportunity for him to change direction in his work life. To say it's not good timing would be an understatement. However, I said that I'm glad for him. "It's not easy, love, but we'll manage."

Don't I sound good and virtuous, Mary? The truth is, I cried and cried when I was alone. We can barely afford groceries, and I'm eating bird peanuts from the pet shop to fill me up between meals. I don't know how we'll cope, but somehow, we'll have to.

Isn't that right, Mary? Tell me it's going to be OK.

CHAPTER 6

Dear Mary,

Well, we've moved again. This time to Wiltshire, which we like very much. It's another English shire, but we aren't so out in the country, and there seems to be a bit more going on.

And, after much discussion and deliberation, Christopher has taken the plunge and signed up to study journalism and radio at Chippenham College as a mature student.

He's so enthusiastic about his studies. Money is tight, so he's doing two years in one, but Christopher has his *Joi de vivre* back, and is doing well. He doesn't mind being a 27-year-old in a class of teenagers, and I'm proud of him.

So, he's happy, but we don't see much of each other. And I'm finding life hard. I'm so tired. Timothy still doesn't sleep well. Some nights, when I've not managed to get much sleep, Christopher takes him off in the early hours in the car for a three- or four-hour drive, allowing me to finally get some rest. Timothy sleeps well in the car, and Christopher is seeing a lot of Wiltshire (although most of it is in the dark). Then, just as the sun is rising, he's back, hands the now-very-much-awake baby over to me, and gets ready to go off to college.

Tim doesn't tolerate solids of any sort. He's over a year old now, and still only on breast milk. He will eat "normal" food with relish, but then screams in pain for hours afterwards. The doctor thinks he has an "immature gut." He's often sick, with fevers and unexplained rashes, and has two daytime naps of only half an hour each. It's exhausting and unrelenting.

The doctor has suggested that he's a "high-needs" baby and has given me some literature on what that means.

Timmy is such a gorgeous little chap though, with the sweetest smile and happy nature, and looks so much like his father. I simply love him more than I can say. But still, I'm so very tired.

We sleep in separate rooms now. Mary, did I mention this? Christopher and me. He needs his sleep with all the studying he has to do.

But I'm sure it will only be for a season. After all, "this too shall pass," so they say.

Dear Mary,

Where is the time going? I'm sitting on the floor, surrounded by toys, watching two-year-old Timothy dancing around the room to his favorite song. He loves music and has so much energy!

Go, go, go like the Energizer Bunny.

"Mummy, I extwemely hungwy," he exclaims, grabbing my hand and pumping it up and down mercilessly. "My tummy is distwessed with hungwiness, please." My other hand has been grabbed and thumped repeatedly on the sofa.

He comes out with such big words, that he has Christopher and me bursting out with laughter. Christopher has nicknamed him the "Little Professor." He's such a happy little chap, so sweet and earnest, but demands constant, all-consuming attention.

I don't dare take my eyes off him for a moment, and he doesn't like me out of his sight for a second. I dare not even close the bathroom door, which has made for some interesting and often hilarious conversations while on the loo!

But when we go out, he clings to me like a koala bear and hates people to look at him, hiding his little face in my neck and growling at them if they say hello. Is that normal, Mary? Because for my boy to find the world outside our home so scary and uncomfortable doesn't seem right. I know there is shyness, but this is something else completely.

I'm also learning to be extremely thick skinned because the staff at our local grocery store is very disapproving of me and the way I treat Timmy. But I just ignore them now.

You see, Timothy loves to unpack the tins off the shelf and line them up all in a row down the aisle. If I try to stop him, he makes such a fuss, arches his back, and screams and screams right there on the shop floor, thrashing about. I can't even pick him up; he won't have it. I just have to wait till he calms down. The staff does not approve, but I'm learning not to care.

So, I just leave him, and when he's finished lining up the tins, I quickly pack them back on the shelf as best I can, while Timmy starts looking for the next thing to do.

I only go to the shops now if I'm desperate. Christopher does the shopping most of the time, armed with a scrawled list he gets mostly right, while I stay home with Timmy. It's so much easier that way. Anyway, Timmy hates riding in the car during daylight, and screams and fights at being strapped into his car seat. And then, when he does go with us, he usually vomits on even short journeys if he's recently eaten.

Is it no surprise that we have no social life! It's just too difficult, too exhausting even to contemplate.

Christopher went out partying with a friend the other night—an old school friend whom he hadn't seen for ages. Even if we could afford a babysitter, there would be hell to pay if we left Timothy.

So, when Christopher was invited out, I thought it would be mean to veto it. But he came home with lipstick on his sleeve. I mean how close do you have to be to smear lipstick all over a man's shoulder?

When I asked about it, he laughed and said there were so many people dancing all around him. But it has really disturbed me. Do you think I'm being unreasonable? I mean, we hardly have time for each other anymore, and we can't go out together. I'm really upset. Should I be worried? I'm so tired all the time, which makes me so grumpy and short-tempered.

And yes, we still sleep apart....

Dear Mary,

Oh my goodness, where does he get it from? This child is so fastidious! I was trying to play "mud pies" with him today, trying to get him out in the garden, messing around getting a bit dirty. Isn't that what you are supposed to do with your children? Well, he hated the feel of the mud and held his hand away from him and said, "Disgusting, Mummy, disgusting."

He was positively offended that I would actually do this on purpose! He hates any dirt on his clothes, and if even a little food or something gets on his fingers, he holds them away from him and insists I wash them immediately. It doesn't help that my mother-in-law is a "neat freak," so I always joke that this odd behavior must be from Christopher's side of the family.

He's three now, Mary. My lovely boy is slowly growing up, and at the moment, he has two favorite things: Soft Play and Star Wars.

Yes, Star Wars! We often go to the Woolworths' toy section when it's quiet, just to pass the time. They are constantly playing clips of Star Wars on a big screen, and he's absolutely fascinated. He would stand and stare all day if I let him. He stares at the posters, he loves the little figures, and as for the light sabers… of course he has one, and it has given him hours and hours of entertainment.

Then there is the Soft Play area. We were running about there the other day (Hour after hour because he never gets tired!), when a woman very rudely commanded us to leave that area, as it was only for under fives.

I explained that he was only three, but she didn't believe me. I knew that he was big for his age but hadn't considered he looked that different. Well, I wasn't having my boy kicked out, so we locked horns, and I won.

But from now on I'm taking his birth certificate around with me to prove he has as much right to be there as any other little boy. It makes me a little sad that he's only interested in two things. But I'm determined that he'll at least have the opportunity to enjoy them both in equal measure. No one must cross me when it comes to my son. No one.

CHAPTER 7

Dear Mary,

We have bought a house! Can you believe it? Christopher did so well at college, that he even won a meritorious award. He passed all the exams and tried to get into journalism, doing some unpaid freelance work to build a portfolio, but it hasn't been easy. So, instead, he's now working in public relations, and he really enjoys it.

And, I do some waitressing in the evenings for extra money. But we've done it! We have a little (very little) home of our own, and I'm so thrilled.

Timothy loves me reading to him. He acts out the exciting bits, jumping on the sofa, flinging cushions about, swinging his light sabre back and forth.

He's really not a sit-down sort of child at all. But he's only waking once or twice a night now. It's slowly getting better, thank goodness, because I am absolutely exhausted.

I didn't know you could get this tired and keep going. You just have to; you push and push yourself, and then when you think you can't go on anymore, you push yourself again.

But what can you do? We only half joke about trying to find out how to take Timmy's batteries out so that we might have a break because it's so relentless.

Christopher is working really hard at his job. The moment he gets home though, I leave for the restaurant. Ships passing in the night….

I tried taking Timothy to nursery. Actually, I've tried a few times, but he seems terrified of everything: the children, the teachers, the hubbub generally. In fact, with the last one I couldn't even get him into the building!

But then I found a little Steiner kindergarten called Hollyhocks. And it's very special because he will go as long as I go with him (and stay close). The kindergarten staff doesn't mind. There's a woman there called Suzie who speaks ever so softly and gently to him, and he immediately took to her. They follow a predictable routine, which we have discovered is very important, and they allow a lot of running around, both inside and out.

As long as Timothy knows I'm there, sitting in the corner, he's happy to stay.

Phew! What a relief. I even manage to get some reading of my own done some days. Yes, Mary, during those brief hours I actually get to do something for myself again.

Dear Mary,

I have to know God more. If only I could be sure that He loved me like the Bible says, I would be comforted. I don't think anyone else does, except Christopher.

I've just come out of the hospital. Timothy's birth caused some damage, and I've had to have corrective surgery at Bath Hospital. Having been assessed, the doctor said I wouldn't be able to carry another baby to term and suggested that I have a hysterectomy.

Lying there, in one of those undignified gowns, I felt nervous and vulnerable. The medics stood beside my bed discussing my internals as though I wasn't there.

Then my surgeon confronted me with a consent form and pen, asserting that I needed the procedure. When I refused, he claimed in a tone of extreme irritation that I was wasting NHS (National Health Services) money, as I'd have to have surgery a second time at some point in the future.

But I hadn't realized till that moment just how much I really wanted another child. Our family didn't feel complete. And right then and there I realized I wasn't ready to close that door yet, despite what the medical people said.

So, I didn't sign. It was awful knowing that the man who was furious with me was about to perform the surgery, but as I said when Timothy was born, I was a different person now. I wasn't signing it, and that was that.

Christopher's parents came over to look after Timothy while I was in the hospital but inexplicably left on the day I was due home.

They said, "We can't be expected to do everything; her own family can help as well, you know."

But my mother wouldn't come; she never could, always having something more important going on. My sister came with her three children, as I was in bed and barely able to move. Poor Timmy didn't eat for three days, as she just cooked what she wanted, and if he wouldn't eat it, well that was tough. And of course, he wouldn't eat it. It hadn't been made by me—the usual, familiar food, in the correct pot, at the correct time of day.

His whole routine was upside down, so he withdrew into himself miserably. He sat on my bed, while I lay there and read to him, hour after hour.

I'm a strong person, but I felt terrible, and it was getting worse. I talked to my sister, and begged her to be kinder to Timothy, to cook him something that he would like, and do some activities with him.

Our relationship has always been fractious, and for the most part, it's been based on me looking after her through the many dramas and crises she has found herself in. So, when the roles were reversed, it didn't sit well. She was unused to being the caregiver and had little patience for it.

She lost her temper, called Timothy a spoiled brat, and grabbed him to drag him from my bed. We had a momentary tug-of-war before she stormed out, packed up, and left with her children in a taxi!

As the day went on I got weaker and weaker, and that night when Christopher got home, I got up to have a bath, and suddenly there was a whoosh, and blood just poured out of me. Christopher got me to the hospital fast. We were both terrified but trying to stay calm because of Timothy. This really was something completely out of his routine and comfort zone.

It transpired that I had been hemorrhaging, but the blood was pooling inside, so it was undetected, and I was going into shock. That night in the hospital bed, with the blood dripping into my body, I think I turned a corner in my mind.

I was confronted with the possibility that I might have died. And all I could think about was what would happen to Timothy if I weren't there. How would he cope, what would he do, how on earth would Christopher look after him?

I would like to say, Mary, that I was comforted with the response I had to these questions, but I wasn't. There were no good answers, no good solutions. They wouldn't cope. They would go to pieces and perhaps never recover.

They needed me, and I needed to be healthy and strong for them. And I knew only God could help, and I needed to get serious with Him.

So, I resolved to get serious with my Christian faith, and although the nurses gave me sleeping medication, I didn't sleep a wink that night.

CHAPTER 8

Dear Mary,

Well, we have moved again. I may have to stop counting soon because I think we are onto our sixth house already. Anyway, this is the third one that we have owned and is in a small town called Bradford on Avon. Parts of the town are rather beautiful and very old. Older than anything I ever saw in South Africa. The UK has many flaws, but an abundance of timeworn and ancient buildings isn't one of them.

Our house is a mid-terrace (not that ancient thankfully) and not very big, but it's ours and it's much closer to Timothy's kindergarten, as well as a wonderful park in Bath, which is a short drive away. Timothy will be five soon, although he looks more like a seven-year-old.

We have such fun in the park! He takes off like a bat out of hell the moment we arrive, and flies around in ecstasy for hours, running from one piece of equipment to another. If nothing else, he keeps me fit!

But he doesn't play with the other children much. I can see he wants to, but somehow he can't seem to "break in." Sometimes it makes him very distressed, and it makes me very sad to watch.

You know, Mary, I think something's up with Timothy. He's not like the other children; and it's not my fault, although everybody seems to think it is.

The other day, we were at a home education group that I joined. I haven't mentioned this before, but we're trying to home educate Timothy. It's legal here in the UK to do this. As long as you can demonstrate that your child is getting an education, you don't necessarily have to send them to school. And with Timothy being the way he is, there's no way that he could go to school.

They start school here in the UK at four, but the kindergarten has said they will take him until he is six, which means that from five onwards he's technically being home educated. I'm not a teacher, and I know nothing about teaching, but I know that to send him to school now would be to break him and would be the most unkind thing I could do to my son.

Anyway, we were at this group, all sitting at various tables, with activities set out. Now Timothy doesn't like to try anything new, especially if he thinks he may not do it perfectly.

One of the mums at the table noticed and blamed me. "You must be frightening him," she accused. "He's obviously afraid of making mistakes. You shouldn't be so harsh with him."

I didn't respond, I never do; but it's so unfair, the assumptions people make. And I seem to be getting it more and more. Christopher's parents assumed that his sleeping and eating issues were my fault, and I should have "dealt with them" early on.

My sister rolls her eyes and says (now that we are back on speaking terms), "I don't know where you get the patience from. I'd give him a good spanking." And my parents (who we hardly ever see) are also of the "good hiding" opinion.

So, if I'm not being too patient, I'm being too harsh! But it breaks my heart, because he's the sweetest, gentlest, most sensitive little boy.

So very, very vulnerable, and I'm frightened for him. He needs to be understood, and only Christopher and I seem to "get" him. People are so critical. Nobody else loves him, and it makes me sad.

So, I pray. I pray a lot. I've even found some wonderful books, such as *The Power of a Praying Wife,* and *The Power of a Praying Parent.* They're really helping me, and I'm praying these prayers every day.

But, Mary, I must admit that I think there's something up with Timothy. Something about him that isn't quite compatible with the world in which he lives.

Dear Mary,

I can't write much today because I'm too upset. You see, I've been reading an article in a magazine, and it was as though the author was describing my son.

One thing about his Star Wars passion is that it gives me some downtime. Timothy may be bouncing off the walls, leaping about fighting imaginary foes with his light sabre, but his complete concentration is on the TV screen. He loves to watch that movie! I don't have any ornaments or breakables in my house anymore, that's for sure!

Oh, the joy of sitting down with a nice cup of tea and a magazine! A magazine, which had an article that caught my eye. I started to read it, but soon my dread was rising. It was as if the writer was talking about Timothy, and only Timothy; but that can't be right because the article is talking about a child with Asperger's Syndrome.

It's an autism spectrum disorder, on the higher functioning end of the spectrum. He was explaining about their problems with social interaction and communication issues. He talked about restricted ranges of interest, a need for structure and routine, sensory issues, and emotional outbursts. And, oh Mary, he might as well have titled the article: "Everything you need to know to understand Timothy."

On and on he went, describing our lives as though he had lived with us these past six years. He explained how, unlike other forms of autism, children with Asperger's often didn't have difficulties in language, even demonstrating precocious vocabularies at times.

The article finished by talking about the problems "aspies" have as they grow up. Social isolation and loneliness, emotional meltdowns, higher risk of suicide, learning difficulties, and on and on.

I know that there are issues, of course I do, but I really hoped that with the right support, love, and encouragement, he would somehow grow out of them. But this article has put me straight on that. He is on the autistic spectrum, no doubt about it.

I can't bear to write anymore, Mary; it's too much. My lovely Timmy. Oh God, why? Why us, and why him?

Dear Mary,

I had to tell Christopher. I didn't know how he would take it; he's not in a good place right now. He can barely crack a smile until he's had a couple of beers when he comes home from work at night.

So, I told him last night, and it didn't go well. I was shaking and holding back the tears, but he just totally dismissed it. He said, "Rubbish, that's rubbish my darling. He's just a particularly sensitive boy; he'll be fine."

I know he adores Timmy and can't bear to even contemplate that anything might be wrong with his beloved son. But I persevered, "Well what about school? He's supposed to be going now, you know. The kindergarten won't have him for much longer.

You know as well as I do that we can't send him to school. In fact, we're already home educating him. No, that's not right. I'm already home educating him."

"No, no, he's not ready for school yet. He just needs a little time. Let's just wait and see."

"Not ready"! That's a typical English understatement if ever there was one. When I accused him of sticking his head in the sand, he accused me of being negative and a pessimist.

I started shouting and crying, "You never talk to me! I know that there's something wrong at work, I know we have money problems, I know you are depressed. And I'm bloody tired, and I can't cope anymore. And you just say, 'We'll be fine.' When are you going to take your head out of the sand and admit we have problems? It's not fine; it's not even close to fine! What the hell are we going to do, Christopher?"

I'm ashamed to admit it, Mary, but I was sobbing by this stage. Then Timmy's little face appeared in the doorway, looking worried. Christopher shot me a look, then cheerfully exclaimed, "Time for us to play soldiers, big boy! Let's go!"

How am I supposed to deal with all of this, when he won't even admit that anything is wrong? Well, there's only one thing I can do—keep praying.

CHAPTER 9

Dear Mary,

I'm waitressing mornings now at a really grand hotel called Lucknam Park near Bath. It's so beautiful there. Phew! Perhaps one day I'll be the one being served, instead of doing the serving! Oh, wouldn't that be lovely!

Bradford on Avon has a nice swimming pool, so we arranged for Timothy to take swimming lessons, which he loves, as the class is very small. But he won't put his head under water for anything! He just refuses point-blank to do it. However, his teacher is really relaxed about this and just laughs. What a relief!

Timothy has been asking for a baby brother, and I must admit, Mary, I really, really want him to have a sibling. The thought of him being on his own when we die fills me with dread. I don't want him to be an only child. If he had a brother or sister, at least he or she could be by his side as he gets older. To help him when possible, to shield him from the worst of the world.

So, every night Timmy prays for a brother. "But God may give you a sister, darling."

"No," he insisted, "God will send me a brother." He is so determined, what can I say?

Are we reconciled about Timothy being on the autism spectrum? I don't know. Christopher and I don't talk very much about it. Or about anything else, to be honest. For someone who works in the communications business, Christopher is sometimes a very lousy communicator.

But perhaps our desire to have another child is evidence of a sort that we know Timothy is going to need some help and support when we're gone. Is that admitting that he's autistic? I don't know, but we've been trying for a baby in a very spirited fashion.

In fact, we have even applied for fertility treatment because I'm having problems conceiving. We don't know if NHS will agree to it, but it's worth a try. And worth praying about.

Dear Mary,

Can you believe it? The NHS doctor has agreed to give me fertility treatment! I thought with my history, they would refuse, but I'm on Clomid now, so let's hope and pray....

Dear Mary,

Yes! Yes! Yes! I'm pregnant! I'm so excited! Christopher's away, but I can't wait to tell him! Oh, I hope it will be all OK.

Dear Mary,

I was taught that when you're a Christian, nothing happens to you that God doesn't allow.

So why is He punishing me, Mary? What did I do? It's so hard to believe that He loves me but allows this to happen. I don't understand.

Timothy and I walked down all the little alleyways that take us to town. He was enjoying being out in the sunshine, chatting happily about Star Wars, and then suddenly I was bleeding. I was bleeding a lot. We managed somehow to get back home, and I phoned the hospital and was whisked in to see the doctor.

The news was terrible: "You've had a spontaneous abortion," the doctor explained. "An early miscarriage. I'm afraid there's nothing to be done. You are almost 35, and that, together with a uterine prolapse, and your medical history, indicates very little chance of a positive outcome. So, we've decided to discontinue your fertility treatment."

He glanced at Timothy, rummaging through a box of toys in the corner: "You have a lovely little boy here; just enjoy him."

He smiled at me, but I'm afraid, Mary, I didn't smile back. Am I ungrateful? Should I give up?

I do thank God for Timothy, but my heart is breaking for the baby I've just lost.

Last night, when Timothy prayed for a little brother again, I tried, really gently, to tell him what the doctor had said, that mummy can't have any more babies.

But he just smiled happily and said, "No Mummy, not a baby; a brother. God's going to give me a brother."

And I was lost for words.

Dear Mary,

It's all been too much for Christopher. Recently his boss called me and asked, "Where's Christopher?" I replied, "What do you mean 'Where is he?' Isn't he there?" He wasn't. He hadn't shown up for work. But he'd left home as usual that morning.

Later that day I heard from him. He was in Bournemouth, down on the south coast. He'd boarded his train as usual, but instead of getting off the train at Bath, he'd stayed on it all the way until it terminated at Bournemouth. He'd disembarked there, found a bench, and stared out to sea all day.

He's worried about Timothy, we've lost the baby, we have financial troubles (When haven't we?), and he's just found out that his boss is about to file for bankruptcy (and he will be out of a job again). Something inside of him has broken. My poor Hubs; it's all just too much.

Dear Mary,
Christopher's had what can only really be described as a nervous breakdown. The doctors have booked him off work indefinitely, and they have prescribed Prozac. He has been signed up for a weekly course of cognitive behavior therapy at Chippenham Hospital.

He wanders sleeplessly around the house at night. They have prescribed sleeping pills for him, but will only give him two at a time, as his psychologist considers him a suicide risk.

Oh, it's agonizing to watch my husband, who was once full of fun and laughter, reduced to such a state.

Well, this is not going to break us. We simply can't give up. We're going to get through this somehow.

Isaiah 41:10 says: "Fear not, for I am with you; be not dismayed, for I am your God. I will strengthen you, yes, I will help you, I will uphold you with My righteous right hand."

So, I'm going to grit my teeth, and pray, and trust God to help us. We have to get back to a normal life somehow. We just have to!

Dear Mary,
Well, we're all getting on OK. Tim enjoys having his dad at home, although Christopher sleeps a lot in the day.

These past ten months have been strange. Christopher is alright, but not himself somehow. The cognitive behavior therapy has been very helpful; he's really taken it on board, and is working hard through the assignments that he's been sent.

The whole process seems to work by peeling away the layers of your personality through questioning until you get to your core beliefs. Then you challenge them, change them, and start to rebuild them. And, we have discovered that Christopher's core beliefs were urgently in need of a major overhaul.

Dear Mary,

Christopher has recovered enough to start working again but can't handle both work and our home life at the same time. So, he's found a job out of town, and is staying in a little bedsit near his office, only coming home on the weekends.

Timothy misses his dad so much. Many nights I sit with him while he weeps and weeps, begging for his daddy to come home. After getting him settled, I go to bed and cry myself to sleep, thinking the same thing.

Oh Mary, if I didn't have God, I don't know how I'd cope. When Christopher first moved out, almost a year ago now, things were OK. He phoned every evening to say goodnight to Timothy and have a little chat with me. But recently things have begun to change. He seems to have stopped noticing me, acknowledging me.

One night after speaking to his dad, Timothy handed the phone to me, but Christopher had already hung up. He'd forgotten to talk to me. After that, I never knew if he would talk to me or not. Mostly he did, but not always. I felt as though I'd become invisible to him, an incidental person in his life.

It was his birthday, and he went out to dinner with his brother and sister-in-law. I wasn't invited. I was just sitting here, wondering what on earth was going on.

Is he planning to leave me?

Does his family know something I don't? Is there someone else? This can't be normal. I've just spent the last hour on the phone to The Samaritans. The chap there said we need to go to marriage counseling, but I've investigated it, and it's too expensive.

Somewhere along the way, he's stopped loving me. Is that what I'm facing? He has fixed himself up, and in doing so, I wonder—has he decided that he doesn't want me anymore?

Do I have to admit finally, that my husband no longer loves me? How do you make someone love you again? If there was anything I could do, I would do it, but I'm at a loss. I've just got to keep praying.

God has just got to help me.

Dear Mary,

When Christopher came home for the weekend, Timmy was so happy to see him, and there were big hugs, but he barely acknowledged me. I felt like the child minder, not his wife.

You know, Mary, I've had enough! I am so angry, after everything we've gone through, he treats me like this. When Timothy was playing in his room, I confronted him, and all hell broke loose. Accusations and recriminations, tears and drama, but at least we talked. Finally, we talked.

I remember the early days, when Christopher's eyes had sparkled with good humor and love when he looked at me. The way he made me laugh! How he ran up and down the stairs with warm water while I was in labor. The gentle way he knelt on the floor to dry my feet.

I remembered the adoration in his eyes the first time he'd held Timothy. The way he'd driven him around for hours and hours all those mornings so I could sleep. Was that love and laughter still there?

Was it even worth the effort to even try to find out?

Last night, I was having a bath and I prayed, "Lord, may I divorce him please? I've gone off him big time."

But the answer came swift and short: *"No."*

I felt crushed and angry, but through my tears I heard the still, small voice of the Lord whisper, *"Things will be better than before."*

CHAPTER 10

Dear Mary,

I've started reading *The Power of a Praying Wife* from the beginning again, and I'm praying my heart out! But sometimes it's through gritted teeth.

I really, really don't feel like it some days. I just want to call down lightning instead. That would be a lot easier and a lot more satisfying.

But I force myself to reread the first chapter. Especially the "What about me?" bit! *Aargh!* It's so hard!

There is one chapter where it talks about how to pray for his fears. And I said, "I have fears too, you know, but no one is praying for me." And suddenly I heard the words: *"I'm listening."*

So, I prayed the prayer for me as well. That's when I started praying for myself; when I found prayers that were relevant.

Dear Mary,

Christopher used to be an atheist. Some years back he had kidney stones and was on morphine and while drugged up to his eyeballs because of the pain, he made an amazing discovery: even though he was heavily sedated, couldn't speak much or move, a small part of him inside was still stone cold sober; coherent, in control, and lucid.

He says that was the day he discovered his soul. He's not an atheist anymore.

Then recently, I was waitressing at a freemason dinner (they are rubbish tippers), and I had to go down to the cellar. The other waitresses were terrified, because there were stories of it being haunted. What nonsense. So, I went down instead. It was freezing down there, and there was an oppressive atmosphere.

Oh Mary, I was praying my socks off going down the stairs, and I said, "Don't you dare touch me, don't you dare," over and over again. And it didn't. I found what I needed, and that was that.

When I got home that night, Christopher said, "Did something strange happen to you at 8 o'clock tonight?" Well this was the time I was in the cellar. Apparently, at that same time, Christopher was sitting on Tim's bed, with his door open, and saw a figure appear at the top of the stairs.

He looked like a tramp, but stared at Christopher with what he called "malignant hatred." This apparition appeared for just a moment. But it certainly got Christopher's attention. I'm not sure what it's all about, but Christopher now knows (and believes) that there are evil spirits out there.

Did that help in the changes that have happened recently? I don't know, but we've been talking a lot more than we have in years, and have decided that our priorities have been out of order, and we have to change.

We both have some apologizing and forgiving to do, and some new commitments to make. We can't afford marriage counseling, but we are going through a book by Dr. Phil, which is really helping to give us some insight into how to mend our marriage.

As you know Mary, forgiveness is not my strong point; but I'm trying my best, and, of course, praying a lot.

But that's not even the best news. We were in the car the other day, and it was quite a long trip, so I was reading to Timmy, to keep him alert. If he falls asleep and wakes up in the car, he has a complete meltdown. He thrashes about and arches his back. Now that he's quite big, it's even harder to deal with.

We had been reading through *The Chronicles of Narnia* series and were towards the end of "The Last Battle." As I was reading, I noticed Christopher wiping tears away from his eyes.

Later, over coffee, I asked him about it.

"When you were reading the bit about the dwarves in the shed, and how Aslan said they couldn't be taken out, because they wouldn't be taken in, I realized that they were in their own hell and Aslan couldn't help them. It was like scales falling from my eyes; like the world went from black and white to color. And that's when I realized that there is a God, and I need Him."

Christopher, my husband, accepted Jesus right there in the coffee shop!

Mary, there's a new peace about him now. He has decided to give up his flat, move back home, and commute to work. He said he had decided to put Timothy and me ahead of himself from now on. We had a little ceremony at home to renew our marriage vows.

I am so, so happy! And Timmy's so excited to have Daddy back home again. God is really answering my prayers. Isn't it wonderful?

Oh yes! There's more! You know I accused him of being like Data from Star Trek? He seemed to have no feelings, no empathy. Anyway, he thinks the antidepressants did this and changed his personality, so he's thrown them all away!

I freaked out and said he needed to wean himself slowly or the withdrawals would be terrible, but he was adamant. He had been having dreadful withdrawal symptoms, and said it felt like there was huge pressure in his head, pushing at the back of his eyes, but he was adamant, so I just kept praying that he'll be OK. That we'll be OK.

CHAPTER 11

Dear Mary,

Ta da! I'm pregnant! Six months in, and all is well! And this time without the need for fertility treatment. *Woohoo!* Can you believe it? I know it's been months since I last wrote, but I've been busy, busy, busy!

Timmy was right—it's a little boy, and Christopher and Timmy have chosen his name: James. Baby Jamie, how beautiful is that? I'm so happy. Our little miracle is due around the same time as our tenth wedding anniversary—towards the end of September.

We've had to sell our house, as we just can't keep up the mortgage payments as well as pay off the debt we got into when Christopher was ill. I've been praying over Christopher's work, and our finances, and reading scriptures to stop me from panicking. My favorite scriptures are:

Ephesians 4:32— Be kind to one another, tender hearted, forgiving one another, even as God in Christ forgave you.

Proverbs 24:3-4—Through wisdom a house is built, and by understanding it is established; by knowledge the rooms are filled with all precious and pleasant riches.

Luke 12:29-31—Do not seek what you should eat or what you should drink, nor have an anxious mind. For all these things the nations of the world seek after, and your Father knows that you need these things. But seek the kingdom of God, and all these things shall be added to you.

Galatians 6:9—Let us not grow weary while doing good, for in due season we shall reap if we do not lose heart.

So, I won't lose heart, no matter what. Which is just as well, because Christopher has been made redundant again!

I've concluded that God must have a better job for him, because I've been praying so hard about it. OK, so I had a wobble at first, admittedly, but I can't afford to get myself in a pickle with baby Jamie on the way, so I'm hoping God will keep helping us.

After all, they said I wouldn't have another baby, and look who's on the way! And I just have to laugh, because Timmy knew all along!

Our present circumstances don't look particularly good, Mary, but in so many ways, we're the happiest we've been in a long, long time.

I'm still homeschooling Timothy, but it's hard work. I'm not a teacher and often don't even know where to start. What I'm doing is teaching him the alphabet, and a few combination vowel sounds. He hates to write and says his hand hurts. So, I'm leaving that for now.

I've discovered that he has a real issue with numbers. We go over and over the most basic arithmetic, but he just seems to "lose" the information. It's very disheartening because we're making no progress there.

Anyway, I haven't time to teach him now. I'm surrounded by boxes, and we'll soon be on to the next chapter of our lives.

Dear Mary,

You may congratulate us. It is 2003, and we're the proud parents of a beautiful baby boy. He arrived unexpectedly via emergency caesarean a month before he was due.

So, I'm shuffling around between boxes and chaos trying to sort things out with baby on the breast, making sandwiches with one hand, and trying to focus on Timmy while he tells me all about the exciting new developments in his Halo game. He alternates between playing that and Star Wars games on a new X-Box that we've contrived to get for him to compensate for the current lack of maternal attention!

Oh dear! One minute I feel deserving of a medal for my incredible maternal gymnastics, and the next minute I'm positively slain to the heart with guilt at what a bad mother I am!

We've moved to a little (cheap!) farmer's cottage just down the road from Christopher's new job in Swindon. Yes, he has a new job, but because our miracle arrived rather sooner than expected, Christopher hasn't been able to take much time off work, especially as he has just started. He's so excited about this company and his work, he keeps saying, "Further up and further in," with great enthusiasm.

Timothy is loving the Xbox. There's a part of one of his games where aliens speak, and their dialogue is interpreted in subtitles. He needs to be able to read the subtitles in order to make choices in the game. So, I'm constantly being summonsed to his room to read out the options, as he's barely progressed beyond ABC.

But, if I'm not changing nappies or nursing on the sofa, simultaneously making a to-do list or shopping list, I'm trying to sort out the chaos in the kitchen and scratch some sort of meal together. So, I told him, "Darling, I simply can't keep dashing upstairs to read your game for you. Look carefully at the letters, and see if you can work it out for yourself."

Then I prayed, "Oh Lord, please help Timothy to read it," before dashing downstairs to scoop up his loudly objecting baby brother.

Well, that was only three weeks ago. And I suddenly noticed him happily playing on his Xbox and asked how it was going.

"It's great, Mummy, I'm reading it now." I was taken aback. "Read it to me, darling." And he did, taking a few moments to work it out, and then reading it perfectly.

You could have knocked me down with a feather. "But how, love?"

"I did what you said," he grinned, delighted at my astonishment.

"If you can read that, you can read books!" I practically squealed with excitement, rushing to his bookcase. Skimming past the graded readers, I found an old battered Enid Blyton, *Shadow, the Sheepdog.*

Opening it up in the middle, I pointed to a chapter and said, "Can you read that?" He glanced at it for a moment, and then read it perfectly.

Can you believe it, Mary? I have all those graded readers in the bookcase, ready to start him on, and he's skipped them all in one go just so he could understand what's happening in his games. He can read! Just like that!

Christopher was so thrilled with the news, he took Timmy to a big book store and said he could have any books he wanted! He spent the whole week's grocery money in one fell swoop—a huge Dorling Kindersley book on the Star Wars Universe, and several others!

I hope that we've just started a lifelong love of books for Timothy. What joy!

CHAPTER 12

Dear Mary,

I can hardly bear to write this. I cringe when I even think about it. The most awful thing happened the other day. We hired Andie, a 19-year-old *au pair* from the Czech Republic, to help me. I was desperate for help so that I could give Timmy more attention.

She didn't like the house— "Too cold," she scolded disapprovingly, as if the Czech Republic is located somewhere in the Caribbean!

She obviously thought that all English homes were large, warm, and luxurious. But our humble, draughty, single-glazed dwelling did little to keep out the chilly October winds.

"Me?" she asked, looking shocked at the sink full of dirty dishes. "Where dishwash?"

She wasn't at all amused when I pointed, smiling, at her. And she could eat! Oh, what an appetite! But I digress. I'd rather talk about anything but what happened next.

At nine weeks, baby James had recovered from the early jaundice, and was a beautiful, pink-cheeked, angel-faced cherub of a baby. I was rocking him with my foot, as he lay crying in his baby chair, the handle secured behind his head, on the old, quarry-tiled floor of the kitchen.

I was making the morning porridge, and Andie, in her favorite pajamas, which had "naughty girl" printed across her backside, was making herself a coffee. "Oh Jimmy," she sighed, "too much cry." And before I could stop her, she had grabbed the handle to give the chair a big swing.

But the baby wasn't strapped in, and as she grabbed the handle and swung the chair into the air, he was flung out and landed face down on the tiles with an awful thud. His face exploded with blood, and the kitchen reverberated with screams. The baby, Andie, and when he came dashing into the room, Timmy. All screaming hysterically.

I was trying to sooth the baby in my arms, holding a dishcloth over his bleeding nose. "It's OK, Timothy. It's OK, love," I said, while shouting at Andie, "Shut up, just shut up!" I rushed the boys into the sitting room, slamming the kitchen door behind me to quiet Andie's wails, and called the hospital.

To cut a long and ghastly story short, he was alright. Sort of. He had a bit of a concussion and slept a lot that day. There was bruising on his little forehead, and his nose bled on and off. We were back home that evening, to be met by a weeping and broken Czech *au pair*, who had apparently spent most of the day on the phone to her mother.

She was utterly terrified of touching the baby after that, and within a few days was back in her Republic. I decided to manage without "help" after that.

CHAPTER 13

Dear Mary,

What with the upheaval of moving, the arrival of the baby, and then the Andie incident, poor Timothy has become a sad, lonely, and withdrawn little boy. I feel so guilty. Christopher tries to compensate by spending as much time with him as possible when he's at home.

There's a place up the road called Roves Farm, which has, amongst other things, a huge straw bale maze of tunnels. Timothy loves it. We go during the quietest times, when the kids are at school, and chase each other through the dark maze, me on my hands and knees barely making it through, with Timothy shouting encouragement from another tunnel. It's dark and a bit scary really, but also great fun.

These are bright flares in what otherwise has become quite a dark world for Timothy. I know that having James was the right thing to do (especially for the future), but it's hard for him because so much of my time is now taken up with the baby.

Another bright moment was when recently, after three years of trying, buckets of patience, and many tears, Timothy finally learned to ride a bike. He's so delighted and proud of himself. Now he cycles up the dust road to the farm, me trotting behind with James in my arms, encouraging him to go ahead and not to worry, that we'll meet him there.

Anything to help him build some level of confidence and independence in the world.

Dear Mary,

Mark has been Timmy's fencing instructor for the past year. He has experience with "special needs" children, and he's wonderful with Timmy. Christopher and I have at least agreed that Timothy has special needs. Christopher is still in denial about how big the challenge is. He doesn't appreciate how different Timothy is to others his age and keeps hoping that the more we protect him, the more we shield him, the more chance he'll have to develop normally. I don't, however, think that's the case. I know he's autistic, and I hate everything about it.

Mark never tries to touch Timothy, shake his hand, or pat his shoulder—things like that. And our son has learned to relax around him.

It was interesting when Timmy put on the fencing mask for the first time. He straightened up, head high, shoulders back, foil up. It was as though it protected him and set him just that little bit free.

Although he seemed to really enjoy the lessons, once they started, it wasn't always easy to coax him out of the car. On days when it took a while, Mark would just "play" with him, rather than teach, and Timmy would slowly unwind, and end up enjoying himself.

Although Mark wanted to introduce Timmy to a class of fencing students, we knew he wouldn't cope with this. What we were doing now was stretching him enough.

After his last session with Mark, being gently prompted, Timmy smiled and said, "Thank you very much, goodbye." Mark's face was a study, as he tried to respond. Whispering incredulously to me as we left he said, "I didn't realize he could speak!"

Driving home, I couldn't resist a chuckle. An hour a week, for a whole year, and Timmy had not said a word.

But get him home and talking about Star Wars, and you could be on your fourth cup of tea before he drew breath! Bless him, Mary, I love him so much.

Selective mutism, that's what they call it. I hate that label. It suggests he has a choice, but I've seen him struggle and struggle, and he doesn't have a choice. Sometimes he simply cannot speak, and people get so impatient and upset with him.

I hate autism.

Dear Mary,

Well, we've found a school that will take Timothy. It's a Steiner school, and it's the only one we've found that seems remotely viable. I've been really struggling to home educate and to look after James at the same time. I know, Mary, what did I expect? That it was going to be easy? But the guilt of knowing that Timothy is beginning to languish is eating me away. We have to try this, we have to see if he can cope. Not in a mainstream school. We know that will never work. But in a Steiner school, where they're more tolerant of differences, there may be a chance.

And he's excited, too. He has such high hopes: "I'm going to have friends, and play with them, and go to birthday parties too."

All he ever wants is friends. Because, at the moment, he has none.

Dear Mary,

For the initial three months he only went for two hours, arriving after the class had settled down. He couldn't handle all the hubbub of the children swarming into the school, excited and chattering.

He loved being with other children, but being unable to play ballgames because of his poor coordination, he was rejected in the playground, relegated to having to watch on the sidelines. Alone. Having realized that misbehavior meant staying in the classroom during break time, he began to misbehave on purpose—anything to avoid the constant rejection.

It was even worse when he started staying full days. He spent his breaks wandering around aimlessly. He often sat under a tree and wept. Oh Mary, why did God do this to him? How will he live this life? He simply doesn't have the ability to cope. And how will he grow up and live a life with this relentless dashing of his hopes, this constant heart-rending rejection?

I'm getting to the point where just a dirty look enrages me. And the smallest kindness has me weeping with gratitude. If only I could smash this invisible malignancy that is destroying his life, and somehow set him free.

He seems to just about manage to keep it together at school, but when he gets home he has what we call full-on storms. He flies into violent rages, head-butting the floor, slamming doors, and punching himself in the head from sheer frustration and distress.

There's nothing I can do to comfort him. Finally, he just collapses into an exhausted, sobbing heap, weeping and weeping. He's becoming emaciated again, as he's lost his appetite and has even stopped growing. He complains of having recurring nightmares that he's drowning.

He's not managing with the written work, which is more of an issue, now that he can compare his abilities with the other children. He hasn't the fine motor skills to do the craft activities and sits there mortified and frustrated while the other children breeze through the cutting, pasting, threading, and knitting.

The teacher (who is not at all the kind, gentle, patient person Timothy needs) has referred us to a counselor attached to the school. After a lengthy chat, she said, "You may have to face the fact that Timothy may be the sort of child who will never be able to tolerate a schooling environment. Now you must pay me please; I have another appointment."

We were desperate to try to make this work for our precious boy, so we designed a plan of action with the school, putting certain strategies in place to help him and taking him back for two-hour days. Maybe this will work…maybe.

Dear Mary,

Well, we have moved again. (This is our eighth house, but who's counting?) This time we have moved so that Timothy can be as close to the Steiner school as we can get him.

The people next door to us here in Gloucester are lovely. There are two boys, Mizach and Ischmael, who have made friends with Timothy. They love to come around to our garden and play, as it's the school summer holidays. They spend hours on the trampoline, eating ice lollies and lunch with us, and playing light sabers together. As long as I'm there constantly to supervise, it goes well.

James is a cheerful, laughing, little toddler aged one now, and loves being around the big boys in the garden. He's the sweetest little baby boy, all chubby pink cheeks, baby chatter, and chuckles.

We absolutely adore him. If only he would sleep. If anything, his nights are even worse than Timothy's were. And as you know, Mary, that's saying something.

However, I have an interesting story for you. I wonder what you'll make of it.

These last few months, Timmy developed a lot of health problems. His face was very pale, and his eyes looked bruised with dark shadows. He had recurring fungal infections, constantly complained of painful joints, and most days he seemed to be exhausted.

Rashes and fevers came and went on a regular basis, and he had an almost constant cough and sore throat. His glands often swelled and were painful. If he did even moderate activity, it took him days to recover. He complained of a burning sensation in his stomach, causing him to eat often to ease it.

Stomach pains kept him awake at night. He complained of headaches and feeling achy all over. His gums were swollen and bled a lot, and his tongue was sore.

As you can imagine, I felt frantic with worry, but the doctor couldn't have been more dismissive, inferring that I was being paranoid and overprotective. When I suggested that Timothy might have something like glandular fever, he countered with, "Which one of us has been to medical school?"

However, Mary, you know that I'm not the person I used to be. My respect for medical professionals was never very high, but after becoming a mother it had dropped even lower. So I did some research of my own, and contacted nutritionists and homeopaths, trying to find an answer.

Most suggested that he had coeliacs disease, dairy intolerance, or leaky gut syndrome. Bearing in mind that he was already a fussy eater, and that 90% of his diet included bread, pasta, and dairy, I was desperate to know what to feed him.

It's awful to think that the food you're feeding your child is making him feel even more poorly. But when I tried introducing alternative foods, he just refused them.

Every night while he slept, I knelt by his bed and prayed. I prayed and cried, desperate. I was so afraid he had something like leukemia.

When James woke at night (which was very regularly), I'd sort him out, before coming straight back to Timmy's room. I'd sit on the floor next to his bed, with my hand gently touching his leg, and pray, then sleep a little, and then pray some more.

It's been a lovely warm spring and summer, so I've spent a lot of time in the garden with the boys. I had re-potted our live Christmas tree in early spring, throwing in a bit of fertilizer, and keeping it watered. But to my disappointment, it was slowly dying.

I was staring at it thoughtfully, nursing James, while Timothy played with his figures on the lawn, when I heard the words: *"Lay your hands on that tree and bless it."*

Bless the tree? That's a bit odd, but I said to Timothy, "I think God just told me to bless our Christmas tree!" He just smiled at me and kept on playing.

A few minutes later I had both my hands on that tree (first checking that Mizach and Ischmael's mom wasn't in her garden–I suspect she thinks we're peculiar enough as it is). Then I blessed it in every way I could imagine. I blessed its roots to absorb water and nutrients properly. I prayed that it would be healed of any disease.

And I blessed all its inner bits to work properly (although, I admit, I'm not much of a botanist).

Early the next morning, Timothy started shouting from the garden, "Look, Mummy; come and look!" I dashed out with James wriggling in delight on my hip.

Timothy was laughing and pointing at our Christmas tree, which now had these bright green shoots all over it, each over an inch long. Dozens of them.

We stood there laughing incredulously, and I heard: *"If I can do this for the tree, won't you trust Me to heal Timothy?"*

The first thing I thought was, *But what about all the gluten and dairy issues? What about his diet and his leaky gut?*

And I heard, *"Bless his food, and trust Me."*

Dear Mary,

The thing is, we've always blessed our food, but I suppose it had become a sort of tradition.

Now I started blessing it with real faith and expectation. I prayed that it would be a blessing to his body. And, I blessed his body, that it would be able to digest and absorb the nutrition properly. I tend to pray with my eyes open, and there was Timothy, spoon poised impatiently, desperate to start.

But then I had a picture in my mind of the children of Israel collecting manna—angel food. It contained everything they needed: every vitamin, mineral, oil, everything! They lived on it for ages and were perfectly healthy.

So, I added to my prayer, "I pray that this food will be like manna to our bodies and provide us with all the nutrition we need to make us strong and healthy," by which time Timmy was positively desperate. "In Jesus' name, amen," he concluded loudly, before wolfing down his porridge. Later, he had yogurt, then bread, then spaghetti bolognese. Every time he ate, I blessed the food and his digestive system.

By the end of summer, he was a different boy. Slowly, one by one, the physical problems cleared up. He had color in his cheeks, his gums stopped bleeding, his breath was normal again. And he stopped complaining of pain.

I was so relieved and grateful. What else might God do for us, I wonder?

CHAPTER 14

Dear Mary,

Well another plan's fallen apart. I've taken Tim out of Steiner school. I just couldn't do it. There he was, crouched at the foot of the passenger seat, refusing to get out of the car.

I watched as the other children called out greetings to each other, and walked in pairs and groups, off to their respective classes. And here was Timothy, pleading with tears in his eyes—a pale, anxiety-ridden little boy, hiding on the floor of the car, desperate not to get out.

My little fellow. My beautiful, sad little boy. How could I force him out and then drive off? I couldn't.

"OK, my darling, I'm driving home now. Get on the seat, and put your seat belt on." It was such a relief for both of us. He looked at me, fear still etched onto his pale little face. I knew what he was thinking: *Was this all going happen again tomorrow?*

I smiled and patted his arm. "Sweetheart, I will never again send you to a place where you're so unhappy." I don't know what we're going to do about his education, but nothing can be worth that sort of misery.

When we got home it was party time in the garden. Relieved and lighthearted, Timmy and I danced around gleefully in the warm sunny garden. Soon the hosepipe was out, and the two of us had a wonderful time squealing and squirting each other, while James sat in his sandpit, laughing and clapping his little hands.

Good times from bad.

Dear Mary,

I'm trying to stay positive. This will be our third move in a year! Christopher is doing really well at work and has been promoted, which is lovely. Perhaps he's finally found a job that he can grow into, that can help him fulfill his potential.

He's been transferred to the head office in Northamptonshire, which is a couple of hours from where we were, so we're on the move again (Is that nine houses now?).

I'm so exhausted. James barely sleeps. Our nights are hell, sheer hell. And Christopher and I still don't sleep in the same bed. He sleeps on the sitting room floor to get away from all the noise. Me, however, I'm trapped all night with this little child who is a sweet angel in the day, but awful when the sun goes down.

I haven't slept more than an hour at a time for months. I haven't even seen the house in Peterborough we're moving to. I'm too tired to drive, and Timothy is so sensitive, that we don't want him to have the added stress of a long car journey before it's absolutely necessary.

So, Christopher went to see it and signed up there and then to take it.

Dear Mary,

We're here, the house is nice and big, but it's one of those new homes that seem to be made of cardboard and polystyrene, sitting in a veritable rabbit warren of other houses on a massive estate.

We've been sorting out Timmy's room, putting his books, toys, gadgets, and furniture as close to the usual layout as possible. But he just hates moving so much. And yet we keep having these moves, each one an attempt to try and find a better place for us to live, a better place for my boys to grow up. Each move an act of almost blind hope that this time, finally, we'll find a place where we belong.

Earlier on today, Timmy paced about crying. "It's all wrong, it's all wrong," he protested, tearing at his hair in frustration, before climbing under one of our big sofa cushions and weeping. "Mummy, come and sit," he said.

As he stretched out on the sofa, I put another cushion on top of him and sat on it, his panic subsiding as the heavy pressure helped to calm him down.

We've just about killed ourselves getting his bedroom and the kitchen sorted out. I had to get all the pots and pans unpacked, all the usual cutlery and crockery out, so I could prepare his food in exactly the way it usually is, or he won't eat.

He has no two foods touching, cooked in the right saucepan, served on the correct plates, and eaten with his own cutlery! If ever we dare to be somewhere other than at home during meal times, I have to take his cutlery, my pots, pans, and dishes with me. Timothy insists that food tastes different if cooked in a different pan and therefore won't eat it.

Whereas, Jamie has been happily toddling about, investigating boxes and piles of stuff with interest, mumbling contentedly to himself, seemingly oblivious of all the chaos and stress and happily helping himself to food off our plates. How different can two children be?

It's also amazing how a good stiff shot of whiskey can help you relax.

What a day!

CHAPTER 15

Dear Mary,

Shortly before we left the old house, Christopher came home one evening, poured himself a strong drink, and said, "OK, Deb, let's get him assessed. I've been doing a bit of research, and it's made me feel so sad. But I think you're right; it really does look like autism, doesn't it? I feel like a traitor even saying that. But I can see things aren't going well. Maybe they can help Tim, maybe there's something we can do. My poor boy. I hate this."

There were tears in his eyes. I simply nodded, unable to speak, but the tears rolled down my cheeks.

He will see the pediatric specialist at the autism unit of Peterborough Hospital next month. Here goes….

Dear Mary,

The doctor seems to be a really lovely man—tall and grey, softly spoken, with an Australian accent. He managed to greet Timothy without eye contact or any physical contact, and chatted to him slowly, with pauses, without appearing to be patronizing. It was interesting to see how Timothy managed to cope without getting too anxious. I wish more people knew how to communicate with him like this.

Having gently asked Timothy to wait in another room, he explained that there was no doubt in his mind that my son had Asperger's Syndrome, and that we needed to get him assessed by a speech and language therapist, as well as an occupational therapist.

He noted communication difficulties in the form of a language disorder, stereotypic behaviors, sensory sensitivities, marked difficulties in social reciprocity, mood regulation difficulties, and developmental coordination disorder.

He explained the general principles of behavior modification techniques to manage the "storms" (meltdowns) and "switches" (the tendency to deny success, reject praise, and be reluctant to do tasks that one is capable of).

He spoke about low muscle tone, and how the occupational therapist would address the issue of walking on toes, his weak and unstable joints, as well as how to deal with his sensory processing problems. How it was not viable to expect any progress in handwriting skills, but that a keyboard or voice-activated software should be used instead.

The need to use visual timetables and cues to allow him to work his way through daily tasks was mentioned. And so much more.

It was overwhelming, but he was so kind and gentle, and I just nodded while my heart sank lower and lower.

So, there it is, in black and white for all of us to see. No more doubt...and no more hope.

I hate autism.

Dear Mary,

The doctor made an appointment for us to meet an occupational therapist. I was desperate to see her because I wanted her to tell me how to fix things. How to overcome the issues that Timothy was experiencing. How to put things right!

So, after she had chatted and assessed Timothy, I said, "Inside he's fine. He just needs to have these issues fixed. These issues that are making life so difficult for him."

She said, "Tim is not fine. He is far from fine. You're in denial, Mrs. McDermott. Your son has autism. It's time to accept his disability; accept that it's just a part of who he is. And, of course, there is no cure. And because of that, you need to learn how to make friends with autism. It's simply who he is."

Who he is? That is who he is? Get over it. Deal with it. Accept it. Make friends with it.

Never!

Dear Mary,

I don't know how to bear it. And I don't really know where to start.

Even now as I'm writing this, I can't stop crying. The speech and language therapists who are working with Timothy have just visited. They were talking to me about him (it's not good news, poor boy, no wonder he's struggled so much) when one of them looked at James and suddenly laughed, saying, "Isn't it funny how autistic children love trains?"

Now James does indeed love his trains. We have a huge, wooden Thomas the Tank Engine set with miles of track and dozens of engines and coaches that we constantly build and re-build, and James had been quietly playing with it at our feet.

I was thunderstruck (lots of children love train sets; it doesn't mean they're autistic). "Autistic? He's not autistic."

She looked at me surprised, then with some sympathy. "Ah well, perhaps you should have him assessed. He shows a number of distinctly autistic characteristics."

What! Oh, dear God, no, not my Jamie! As I stared at his little golden head, bent over his trains, she continued, "He doesn't talk much, does he?"

A fist of ice rammed into my gut as I looked back at the therapists, giving each other knowing looks. "No, not much. I'd thought perhaps he was just a late starter. He'll be three next month."

Nods. No smiles now. "Look, I'll just write a little report and give it to the pediatrician. You make an appointment with his secretary. No need to go through your doctor. OK?"

And that's all I remember. I must have seen them out. But Timothy was tired and stressed, and I had to stick to the routine. Lunch next. Big smiles. Happy talk. Big smiles. Make lunch. Routine is everything. Stray from it and reap the storm.

But once Timothy was fed and playing on his Xbox, I sat in the sandpit with James, and I did what they said. I made the appointment—what else could I do?

Dear Mary,

I've been thinking about some of James's recent behavioral changes. Loud or sudden noises really upset him, and he'll then walk around with his hands over his ears. He avoids bright lights, hates wearing clothes, and his eating habits have changed. Then, of course, he hasn't learned to talk yet.

But these seem like minor things compared to Timothy's issues that we've been dealing with.

Then, this afternoon, a delivery man peered over my shoulder while I was signing for a parcel, and seeing James (naked again, as he'd taken to stripping constantly at home) playing with his trains (he plays with nothing else), said, "Yeah, my partner's boy is autistic too. His dad couldn't cope with it all and left them, but he's a lovely little lad."

Oh Mary, it feels like my inner scaffolding is collapsing as I sit at the bottom of the stairs, hugging myself and rocking back and forth.

I feel a deep, almost primal wail rising from inside of me.

But Timothy is standing in the doorway staring at me, frightened. Somehow, I have to keep it together for his sake, for the family's sake. But oh God, it is so hard!

We walk into the kitchen, and I lean my head against a cupboard door, taking slow, deep breaths.

I pour myself a whiskey.

Dear Mary,

I told Christopher that night. He nodded and looked worried but also battered and beaten. "Oh well, see what they say."

And they said he has autism.

Dear Mary,

The report goes something like this: "James is clearly showing significant autism in the area of communication, stereotypic behaviors, social reciprocity, and sensory sensitivities."

And in conversation with the doctor, we talked about James's developmental delays. Although he said we would never know for sure, he did say that it was possible that being dropped on his head by the *au pair* when he was a baby may have been a contributing factor.

I'm going to have to tell Christopher tonight, and I'm dreading it. I suppose he'll tell his parents, and they'll probably accuse me of lying, again.

Dear Mary,

My little baby James is disappearing before my very eyes, and I can't get him back. I just can't bear it, I just can't. I want to lie down and cry, but I've got to keep going. I don't dare change the routine. I'm smiling and acting cheerful, but I feel like I'm dying inside.

But he was alright before. That's what's so upsetting me. He was doing OK. What happened to him?

He loved to smile at people when we were out; now he hides his face.

He used to eat finger food. Now he doesn't even seem to get hungry, and I have to distract him with videos and try to spoon puree into his mouth without him noticing.

He heaves and vomits if there are lumps in his food. He used to show me things. Now it's as if he doesn't really notice that I'm there. I find myself struggling to keep his attention.

He fell the other day, there was blood trickling down his shins, and he didn't even notice. It was as if he felt no pain, or he decided to ignore the pain. Either way it wasn't right.

I want to tell someone. I long to just share the pain, but I can't tell anyone in my family.

Not now while this agony is so raw. I've learned not to share my problems with them. They seem to love the drama, to feed off it somehow.

I still haven't even told them about the baby we lost. I can't bear for my pain to be their entertainment. So, I keep it to myself...and I talk to God.

I still can't believe it. Why our boys? Both of them! My beautiful boys. What am I going to do? How can I go on?

I'm so tired, and I want to stop now. It's just too much. I can't cope. I just can't cope.

Dear Mary,

We've moved to Stilton (home of the famous English cheese of the same name) in Cambridgeshire. Our own house again, no more renting! This is the twelfth time we've moved since we got married, Mary. I have to admit that there's something of the "wanderers" about me and Christopher. Our optimism that "this move will be the one" is never ending.

Oh well, Christopher is working very hard and doing so well at the moment. He's still with the same company but has had a string of promotions recently.

The move was hellish. But it's done. Everything's still chaotic, but Tim's room is sorted and, as always, that's the main thing.

He and James didn't cope very well. There have been storms and dramas. And neither of them is sleeping very well. The melatonin helps Tim a bit, but I don't even bother to give it to James anymore.

It makes no difference at all. He still wakes, kicking and screaming, thrashing about in my bed, on and off all night, as has become the norm now. Christopher has his own room and keeps the door closed so he can't hear the noise.

The promotions have brought with them lots of new opportunities but also a lot more traveling. And he's going away again tomorrow for a whole week!

I don't know how I'll manage. He barely responded when James's diagnosis was confirmed, but I know how he feels. What's the use of going to pieces? What's the use of talking it to death? We simply have to get on with it.

He's plowing all his energy into his job so he can support us all, and so we can survive. He can't afford another breakdown, so I think that emotionally he's just checked out.

Mary, you know what I'm like! I wanted to cry, and rage, and talk, talk, talk! But no, we are in survival mode; he does his job, I do mine. No discussion, no debate, just survival. One day at a time.

I'm so afraid. I'm utterly terrified. You know that famous picture of "The Scream." That's how I feel.

I keep asking for help, but everywhere I turn, a door slams in my face. There is no real help. If only there was just one family member who would care enough for the boys to give them some attention, to help Christopher and me occasionally, we'd be so grateful.

But it never happens; there is only You, Lord. Oh God, I pray that somehow You'll get us through this. That You'll save us.

Dear Mary,

This is interesting: After filling out various questionnaires, we've received funding (from a national charity) to do a Son-Rise program seminar in London.

Christopher has booked a week's holiday to look after the boys (I'll be coming home in the evenings). I don't quite know how it will work without a support network, but perhaps it will help us find some keys to "unlock" our boys, and in doing so, set them free.

Dear Mary,

I am absolutely devastated. We had to cancel, and someone else has taken our place. There's no way Christopher could have managed the boys on his own had I gone. It would have impacted the household like an atomic bomb going off.

I am so disappointed and disheartened, but there was no way I could go. James's behavior is becoming more erratic and out of control, which then impacts on poor Timothy, whose structured and well-ordered world has become turbulent and unpredictable, resulting in huge storms and distressing outbursts.

Home life has become a constant balancing act, trying to see to the needs of both boys, without all hell breaking loose. I am so stressed, and I find myself living for my next whisky, just to keep going.

Another glimmer of hope has flickered and gone out, and I'm so despondent.

Dear Mary,

I've been talking to God. I need His help so badly. I talk to Him all the time these days. He's just got to help us… to help our boys, somehow.

I threw the speech and language therapists out of the house the other day. They were trying to teach James Picture Exchange Communication System (PECS), but he was crying and becoming really distressed.

They just laughed it off, but such fury rose up in me! You know, Mary, how protective I've become. How fierce my attitude is when it comes to my boys.

Most children learn to communicate with lots of praise, applause, and delight. Here was James, messing about with pictures, distraught and confused.

I scooped him up, "You will have to leave," I said, "you needn't come back." They were astonished. "The longer you leave it, the harder this will be for him to learn; he may never gain language. Besides, he'll have to have caregivers, and how can they deal with him if he can't communicate with them?"

Well, I don't care. I won't put him through that again. I suppose I'll get a reputation for being un-cooperative, but the thing is, I just know he'll talk one day.

I want so much more for him than bloody pictures and caregivers! I want him to talk and be normal!

Surely there must be a way. There's got to be better than this! If no one else can help, surely God will?

Dear Mary,

The children's services were preparing to hold a parenting workshop for parents of children with autism, to educate us on how to manage behavior. They wanted to come to the house to video James as part of the workshop. "You'll never be able to video James," I said, "he'll be frightened of a couple of strangers focusing on him. There's no way!"

They countered with, "Oh, everybody says that. But we're just taking a little video of each of the kids. We know how to work with them. We understand these children sometimes better than their parents."

But James wouldn't even come into the room, let alone sit and have a video camera pushed in front of him. Finally, to try and put an end to things, I carried my little three-year-old, frightened boy into the sitting room. The women sat quietly, staring at the floor, so as not to alarm him.

In a flash, he arched his back, fell screaming to the floor, and bolted upstairs. When they realized James wasn't going to cooperate, they sat questioning me instead.

Curious as to what was going on, James crept back downstairs and listened from the bottom step. Our dog, Jess, sat beside him. James stroked Jess's soft fur. One of the women slipped closer. Out of sight, but within earshot, she talked to James about Jess.

He does have a few words that he uses, but only I and, sometimes Christopher, can understand what he's saying. However, in that way, they did finally get their film.

Dear Mary,

I attended the workshop and watched the videos of all the children. Child after autistic child came up on the screen, and then there was James.... He was curled up in a ball on the bottom step of the stairs. He had covered his eyes with his hands, trying his best to talk. He was stark naked.

Until that moment, I hadn't realized how different he was, even from other autistic children. That dose of reality felt like having a bucket of ice water thrown in my face.

Instead of feeling reassured that I wasn't alone anymore, I felt more worried and more isolated than ever before.

CHAPTER 16

Dear Mary,

Timothy is a sad boy. He wrote a poem the other day about heaven. He wrote about how much he longs to be there, to be free, and be with God, and how he doesn't want to live here anymore.

I could hardly breathe when he showed it to me. Of course, I thought of Michael, my brother. I think he had Asperger's too, Mary. I can see it now, when I remember him, and then look at Tim. He just couldn't cope either. And so, he put that gun to his head and shot himself. Oh, how desperate he must've been. It's so awful; I can still hardly bear to think about it.

And now Timothy is thinking about death. He's only 11. What do I do?

You know, Mary, a few weeks ago, I was in the kitchen, and I just froze. I couldn't move. It was some sort of horror that hit me, and I stood there.

Finally, I managed to pour myself a shot of whisky, but I was shaking so much, I spilled it. I drank it straight down. It helped calm me down, so I could remember what I was supposed to do next.

It happened again that afternoon. I put some whisky in my coffee with a bit of sugar, and it was quite nice and just took the edge off my fear and pain.

Then last Saturday, I had two drinks, and I wanted to sit down and cry and cry forever.

But, of course, I couldn't. So, I had another, thinking it might help. But it was one too many, and somehow all the scaffolding that keeps me functioning, working, smiling, moving forward, fell away.

All the pain of my whole life came crashing in around me, and I fell on the floor and cried. And cried. And cried. And not softly, not whimpering or anything like that.

I howled like an animal. Christopher was horrified. He grabbed the boys and left the house, so that they wouldn't see me like that. He phoned from the car to talk to me, but I couldn't talk.

I cried for Michael and the pain he must've felt to kill himself.
I cried for my brother Andrew, killed in a car crash when he was 19.
I cried for my other brother Julian, killed in an accidental shooting in South Africa.
I cried for my lost babies.
I cried for the loneliness of my life, and the strange place our marriage had become.

And most of all I cried for my boys. For the solitary, isolated lives they were living. For all the normal things they would never do. For the futures that were so full of unknowns, for their terrifying vulnerability.

Each of these pains had their own little room in my heart, and normally I could close each door, wedge it shut, and cope. But something about the alcohol had broken through all my barriers, and too much pain came rushing out at once. I felt I would die of pain or go insane!

Dear Mary,

Christopher called and called, and I finally answered. He gave me some time to pull myself together then brought the boys home. I had to try to act normal. Like it was just another day in our terrible, lonely, painful world.

I have become something of an actress these days. I can smile and sound cheerful, and I can laugh and make silly jokes with the children, even though I feel like I am dying inside. I'm actually pretty good at it.

And I'm talking to God a lot. I'm praying and praying for my boys.

But I feel so guilty all the time—that I'm not a very good wife, that I'm a rubbish mother; I try and try, but I just can't seem to do better.

And to be honest, Mary, I don't think I'm really a very nice person. I told Him that I think I'd be much nicer if my life wasn't so darn hard.

The other day I was chatting to Him in the kitchen, and He smiled at me. I can't explain it. But I felt that He did, and it was lovely. And it has made me so happy.

I'm listening to Joyce Meyer every day now. I'm reading *Battlefield of the Mind*. Oh, my goodness, I am being challenged!

If only I'd known all of this before! Thanks to that book, I'm watching my thoughts and words very carefully.

Dear Mary,

Christopher printed off some Christian articles about God and autism. He thought it might be interesting and helpful to me. Well, it certainly got me thinking, but it has made me furious. In fact, I'm seething with rage about it.

Let me explain: The first article was about how God gives "special" children to "special" people to parent. So, I'm supposed to feel good about myself, that I must be an especially nice, sweet, patient, lovely person, for God to decide to send me "special" boys.

Well, thanks so much for that. So, all those wicked women out there, fornicating like there's no tomorrow, are blessed with perfectly healthy children. Seriously weird logic.

Some religious types say we are being punished for our past sins. That's why our children have autism. What? What kind of God would that be? What about forgiveness?

And finally: He's teaching you a lesson, perfecting you. In the movies, it's always the evil guy who kidnaps the child, then calls the parent, saying, "Give me money or the kid gets it." Isn't that the same thing? Imagine God saying, "Listen Mom, you've been a bad girl. I'm going to take your innocent, beautiful child and give him a disorder that ruins his life. That will teach you a lesson!"

I know they are wrong, Mary. That's not my God. He wouldn't do that.

Dear Mary,

What a night! They're never exactly peaceful, but this one was somewhat more eventful than usual.

It was just after midnight. James had finally fallen asleep in my arms, when I saw a shadow at my door.

"Mummy, Mummy!" came Timothy's anxious stage whisper. "What is it darling? What's the mat...?" The words died away as I looked at him. I gasped in horror as I shot up to touch his face. His eyes were swollen like tennis balls; he could barely see out of them.

"What on earth happened?" I asked, trying to keep the panic and horror out of my voice.

"I don't know. I just woke up feeling funny, then I couldn't see." He sounded perplexed and frightened.

It dawned on me… the painkillers. In desperation, I'd given him some ibuprofen before he went to bed because of the constant aches and pains he gets.

He must have had a reaction to the medicine. I flew downstairs to find Christopher. Shaking him awake, I said, "Tim's had a reaction to ibuprofen. You need to take him to a doctor."

Looking at the clock he murmured, "Can't it wait till tomorrow?" Before I could explain, Tim wondered in like some confused alien creature.

Just one look at him, and Christopher leapt out of bed, grabbed coats, and hustled Tim out into the freezing night. My poor Tim.

He had such trouble with aching joints. His joints were unstable and hyper-extending, and after just moderate exercise, they would ache so much that he struggled to sleep. (As if we needed any more problems with sleeping!)

He was in so much pain, then struggling with "restless legs" as well, so I finally decided to give him some anti-inflammatory painkillers, just to give him some respite. Then this….

So, is this what I'm supposed to "embrace"? I should make "friends" with this?

One of the therapists also said to me, "Perhaps you should look at autism as another way of being, instead of hoping to find a cure."

Would she like to be Timothy, I wonder? I hate and despise autism and everything related to it. Oh Lord, how are we going to help our boys? You must have an answer to all this.

I'm looking at my little Jamie sleeping next to me. Why can't I fix them? How can I just sit back and watch as hell unfolds all around us?

I wish it could end; I just want it to all stop. Peace from the hell that our lives have become. I just can't bear to watch my boys suffer anymore.

Finally, Tim and Christopher returned, creeping upstairs to my room.

"He's had a severe allergic reaction. We must never give him ibuprofen again. He's had some antihistamines."

"You'll be OK, big son," he smiled, his arm around Tim's ever-broadening shoulders. "You'll be fine now."

I pulled Tim's covers up and kissed him goodnight, smiling reassuringly at his white, anxious little face, eyes swollen monstrously. My heart was breaking with pity and sadness. He was still in pain, but now he couldn't even take the painkillers. The protective love, combined with the agony of being entirely impotent to help him, just tore me up inside.

"I love you, darling," I whispered. "I love you."

Dear Mary,

James has started to keep his clothes on! Well, it's only a Transformer's Bumblebee costume, but he loves it! We bought it for his birthday, hoping it would encourage him to wear something, and it worked.

It's been six months now, and it's all he'll wear, whether it's around the house or, if by some miracle we can get him outside.

But at least he keeps it on.

Dear Mary,

I phoned the people at Joyce Meyer Ministries a few days ago. They sent me a collection of scriptures about healing. I'm trying to sort this out in my head because I'm confused.

Some people say that healing passed away with the apostles. I know that's not true because God healed Tim's digestive troubles.

So, I know He does heal today. But what is the criteria? I mean, I'm waiting for Him to tell me. They said He already promised healing in the Word, and I don't need to hear from Him each time. But then I don't understand why more people aren't healed. If Isaiah 53:4 really refers to physical healing, surely all Christians would be healed? But they aren't.

I find the Bible so hard to understand. What is literal, and what is metaphorical?

Have I been believing wrongly? What about "nothing happens to a Christian that God doesn't allow"? If that really is the case (and for years I thought it was), well then, I'm stuffed, aren't I?

It sometimes makes me so angry, I want to chuck the whole lot out and become an atheist. But I can't, can I?

Because He's been with me, and helping me, and loving me. I know He has. So, something's wrong. I'm praying about it. I've just got to get some answers because no one else can help me.

Dear Mary,

The funniest thing happened to me today. I've been talking to God again. I was in the car with James, and we were listening to music from Winnie the Pooh. I was telling God that I find the Bible really hard to understand, and I don't have anyone to explain it to me.

For instance, I was reading that bit in Isaiah where it says: "By His stripes we are healed" (53:5). Now, I was taught that is referring to spiritual healing. But it doesn't say that, does it? It just says "healed." But lots of people aren't healed. So, what does it mean?

And straight away a song started on the CD, and it was so weird, because I just knew that God was talking to me through the music. The song was "If It Says So."

And that was my answer: If it says so, then it is so! I think I've been given permission to just take the Bible literally and believe what I see. I'm kind of nervous to do that, in case I make mistakes. But then I suspect more and more that in the past I've been taught a load of rubbish when it comes to the Bible.

So, I'm quite excited about reading it afresh, with new eyes.

Dear Mary,

I was stirring some honey into yet another cup of chamomile tea, when I heard a thump, followed by a furious scream.

I rushed into the sitting room, wincing as little bits of Lego pieces cut into the soles of my feet.

"Jamie darling, are you alright? James?" There he was, curled up under the dining room table, shouting furious expletives in his own language, followed by, "No look me, no look me."

I immediately shied away, knowing that if I continued to look at him he would get himself into even more of a state.

Turning my back, I sat in a chair and stared out the window into the drizzly afternoon. After a while, I risked a quick look over my shoulder. An angry welt snaked across his cheek.

How I longed to hold him in my arms, comfort him, kiss his cheek, wipe away his tears. How I longed for him to lift his arms to me, look to me for comfort, and tell me what happened.

But he wouldn't let me in. He's trapped behind the high prison walls of autism. Locked away in a solitary place.

A place where no love, concern, care, or compassion can penetrate, and where eye contact brings agony. A place where a mother's love dare not show itself.

I forced myself to turn back to the window, waiting for his screams to dwindle to mumbles.

In time, I heard him crawl out from his hiding place. I knew that if I turned and looked at him, fury would drive him back in again. So I sat, quiet and still, my attention on Spencer, the only train James allows me to play with.

He crawled up behind me, and I crashed Spencer into the buffer. "Oh no!" I said. "Those troublesome trucks!"

"No, no, Spesser stong, bith, bath douchou tus." I knew what he was trying to say: "No, no, Spencer is strong! He'll biff and bash those troublesome trucks."

Grabbing Spencer, he smashed them together. Closer now, I saw a purplish bruise on his cheek above the welt. There we sat, playing with Spencer and Steamy, smashing the trucks and the tracks up, rebuilding them, and then doing it again.

I watched his golden head bowed over Steamy, his favorite train. An overwhelming wave of love washed over me. But mine is a love tinged with agony.

My beautiful boy. What will happen to him? Who will understand him? Who will protect him and love him like we do? The world finds him so hard to understand, so difficult to love.

What does life hold for him? Will he ever know how much we love him?

It's getting gloomy now. Oh well, I can soon have my afternoon whisky. And I jolly well need it!

Dear Mary,

Poor Christopher, I wish I was a stronger person, a better person. But he never criticizes me, even though we can't really afford whisky. He knows it's hard and knows that as long as I pace myself (ever since that last disastrous episode, of which I am so ashamed), it gets me through the day.

Dear Mary,

I'm such a wreck! I was holding onto Christopher this morning, begging and pleading with him not to go to work. I'd had such a hell night with James (again), and I didn't want to be left alone with the boys for one more hour, let alone a whole day.

I was begging him and crying, "I can't do it today. I'm so tired; please, please, don't leave me!"

He looked so troubled, but Mary, he had that grim, determined look on his face, and he shook me off, saying, "What would happen then, Deb? How would we make it without money to put a roof over our heads? We live in a perpetual state of crisis. I can't afford to lose this job. If I stayed home today, I would be putting everything at risk. They need to know that they can rely on me and trust me to turn up when I'm supposed to."

I wanted to scream, "I don't care! Just don't leave me!" But he went anyway. I stood there crying, just staring down the driveway.

Is this going to go on for the rest of our lives? Please God help me; I cannot do this anymore.

Dear Mary,

It takes so much of my time, playing with James, trying to connect with him and to stop him from withdrawing further. Then poor Timothy gets neglected and spends hours and hours by himself playing computer games, and I feel even more guilty.

Guilt is a big factor in our lives at the moment, Mary.

And I've given up trying to teach Timothy. His learning difficulties make it so stressful and so disheartening for both of us. And when I do try to spend time with him, James starts withdrawing into his own world more and more.

So, it's with a heavy heart that we've had to accept that Timothy needs an environment where he can learn and have more social interaction. He needs to go to school, and after a great deal of research, I've found one designed especially for children on the autistic spectrum.

I've been in contact with them, but he has to have a Statement of Special Educational Needs before we can even request him attending. This is a legal document, that once created, requires the Local Education Authority (LEA) to provide Timothy with a "suitable" education.

Apparently, to get a Statement, I have to enroll Timothy in a mainstream school for six months, so he can be evaluated.

That's crazy, but I've been in contact with support groups, charities, other parents, and specialists, and they all say the same thing: Mainstream school plus evaluation equals (if you're lucky) a

Statement. There's no way he'd be able to function in, or cope, with that!

Well, we will see, but this is ridiculous!

Dear Mary,

I've compiled reports from the educational psychologist, speech and language specialists, occupational therapist, and the pediatrician, and submitted them to the LEA.

Can you believe this? They wrote back, saying there was no compelling reason for them to consider assessing Timothy. I will make them rue the day they sent me that letter! I will fight these people till I win. I am so furious!

I've been speaking to other parents who have been struggling for years to get their children a Statement, and they have explained that the real issue is funding. The LEA, although bound by law to provide an education for each child according to his needs, will fight tooth and nail to avoid making funds available.

The occupational therapist has suggested we take Timothy to see a private neuro-psychologist, who is the highest authority on the subject in the UK.

Although she has a waiting list of six months, when she read Timothy's reports and spoke to me, she felt his situation was so urgent, she arranged to start seeing him straight away. She also agreed to let us pay in installments, which was a relief, as we wouldn't have been able to afford it otherwise.

People take one look at Timothy—tall, good looking, open face, engaging smile, and then dismiss me as paranoid. They can't see anything wrong with him. We are both constantly being so misunderstood.

But when she met Timothy, and started the six weeks of assessments, I realized immediately that she could see past the obvious and would get to the bottom of Timothy's problems.

Dear Mary,

I'm listening to a teaching from Joyce Meyer called "Beauty for Ashes." It's the most amazing thing; I feel that God is really talking to me personally. I've started writing scriptures down and sticking them all over the kitchen to remind me of what I'm learning.

Dare I hope that God will give Timothy and James beauty for ashes? Will He get us out of the mess that our lives are in?

Dear Mary,

He's asking hard things of me. And I don't like it. I've been getting so happy, and hopeful. Then there are these issues coming up inside me that I keep squashing down. Really, it's not about me, is it? I'm praying about my boys, not me.

But I can have no peace. He keeps bringing it back to me, and those closed doors in my heart. I don't want to go there. I don't want to go to pieces again.

Dear Mary,

I know now what I have to do, but I don't want to do it. I woke up this morning, and it had happened again. I dreamt that I shot my father. Dead. This happens periodically. Last time I dreamt that I pushed him out of a window from a high building and killed him. I know it sounds terrible, but I always wake up feeling relieved that he's gone!

I kept having the scriptures about Jesus healing the brokenhearted come up in my mind, and the doors of my heart opening, and light shining out of them.

I have asked Christopher to help me take half an hour every evening for what I call my "Holy Ghost therapy."

The first evening I said, "OK Lord, the bit about my father. What's it all about?"

And immediately, I remembered a time that he whipped my brother Julian so hard on the back of his legs with a belt, that Julian had huge, bleeding welts.

I felt the fury and rage rise up in me so strongly, and God said, *"Give it to Me. Give it to Me, and let him go. Forgive him."*

Oh, I didn't want to Mary, I really, really didn't want to. I felt I was betraying Julian. It hurt me so much, but I needed to let it go, and forgive my father for that (and lots of other things besides).

But I did it. Because He loved me through it. So, I gave it to Him: all the rage and fury and pain, and I forgave my father.

And Jesus went into that room in my heart and cleared it out till light shone through the open door, and I knew I'd never have to close it again.

It took a few evenings. Lots of issues, and lots of forgiving. I didn't realize I had that many wounds in my heart. But I'm so grateful He was kind enough to deal with them one at a time, or I would've been overwhelmed with it all.

But it's done, and I'm free. He's healed my broken heart. "Beauty for ashes," just like He promised in the Bible.

I'm a bit perplexed that He's doing all this work in me, when I keep praying about the boys. But I'm very grateful. Christopher says I've changed. That's got to be good, I'm sure!

Dear Mary,

I feel I'm getting to know Jesus, and when I read the Bible, He seems real to me now, and it's as though He's sitting here with me.

I've lived my whole life with criticism. Nothing I've ever done has been good enough. But last night while I was reading Romans 8:1, I finally realized that I was actually acceptable to Him.

Christopher and I are a good team, we're doing our best. He does his job, and I do mine. He sleeps in his room, and I'm here with James, dramas all night.

I do get envious of Christopher, but I know he has to go to work and deal with business and the real world all day while I stumble around like a zombie trying to survive with the boys at home. There's no tenderness though.

But last night, while James was doing his "sleeping cherub" impersonation next to me, I was just reading a few scriptures under the duvet with a flashlight, and I knew Jesus was there with me. In my mind's eye, I saw Him take my hand and hold it to His cheek. Then He kissed it, held it in both His hands, and smiled at me.

And my heart just melted. I've been so lonely for so long, but I know I'll never be lonely again, because He is here.

And He likes me, and He thinks I'm OK! I've become so accustomed to having to fight, to fight for everything, with constant criticism. I realize I've been on the defensive forever.

But with Him, I can finally let my defenses down. I can't tell you what it's done to my heart. I find I can love Christopher and the boys so much more because He's always loving me.

Dear Mary,

I've had an awful day. Actually, it's been an awful week. OK, so I'm not going to complain, because Joyce says you can be powerful or pitiful, but you can't be both.

It's funny how I hear her voice in my head these days, telling me off when I get out of line! It's funny, but sometimes it's also irritating, because I want to wallow in my misery occasionally. However, it's just not going to happen with Joyce in my head, taking me into a corner and telling me to straighten up my attitude!

But it's really bad with the boys at the moment. Earlier in the week, Tim was full of enthusiastic plans about writing a book, and how he was going to make friends, and all the things they would do.

He was bouncing off the walls with energy and laughing with excitement. But it makes me so uneasy when he's like this, because it's miles away from reality. We don't leave the house or even see another person from one week to the next. And I'm still fighting with the LEA about his schooling.

And James seems to have withdrawn so much into his own world, the boys don't even see each other much. Just two kids, living completely separate lives in the same house.

I've been off to the level crossing twice this week, watching for trains. I sometimes wish we lived right next to the tracks. James would just sit at the window all day, watching and waiting for the next train. He really does love them that much.

When he gets cranky, and nothing seems to please him, off we go to the level crossing. A few trains later, and he's happy again. But I hate leaving Tim home alone when we do. They've told me not to, because he's not safe to be on his own. No "nous," they said. (I had to look up what it meant: "no practical or common sense.") I wish Christopher was home. I'm really battling.

Dear Mary,

Timothy has suddenly crashed. It was like the atmosphere in the whole house changed. And he became so depressed, so unutterably miserable. He's not sleeping and has lost interest in food. He keeps saying he has no friends and that he has no life and no reason to live.

What can I say to him, Mary? I just keep praying because I'm at a loss, completely helpless, completely useless. So, I pray and pray and pray, all day long.

I don't know how much more I can take. How much longer can we go on like this? I'm sorry, I know it's wicked, but I just want to die. I want to die and take the boys with me.

I just wish that the three of us could go to bed tonight and leave this world. It's just so hard and I'm so tired, and the boys are so unhappy.

I wish we could die. I don't want to do this anymore. I don't think I can.

Dear Mary,

You won't believe what happened last night! It's amazing. I'm so excited! Tim's so excited! It's almost too good to be true. But it is true!

Yesterday was Mother's Day in America (May 14, 2007), and it's a date I will never forget.

We'd had another awful day, and when the boys were finally asleep, I decided to watch some TV and try to relax.

I found this Christian program. There was a group of women, all sitting around chatting (oh, I wish I had some friends like that). Anyway, they were talking about their families, and motherhood, and that sort of thing.

And all about God, which was lovely, because I'm really into God these days.

But then they were talking about what it means to be a mother. They were swapping stories and showing photos.

And I folded. I simply sobbed. The difference between what they were saying and what I was experiencing was like the difference between heaven and hell.

I asked God why He wasn't helping us. Why was Tim having to suffer so much? I told Him, "You are supposed to love my boys. I love them so much, I would die for them." And there was this quiet calm voice in my heart that said, *"I already did."*

Well, that shut me up. But I thought about it a little and said, "The thing is, I don't understand why You did. I mean, why did You bother? How does it help? We're suffering so much here. How does Your death on the cross make any difference?"

He said, *"I'll heal them."*

"I'll heal them, I'll heal them…." I sat there, staring into the fireplace, mulling this over. "I'll heal them."

It was as though all the anxieties and fears, all the burdens I had carried for so long, just disappeared there and then—a huge burden just rolling off me.

And I knew we'd be alright. That our boys were going to be OK after all.

I had peace for the first time in many, many years.

CHAPTER 17

Dear Mary,

Well, what do you think? I'm so happy. Christopher's home from his travels, and Timothy was bouncing around him saying, "Daddy, Daddy, God's going to heal me! God's going to heal James too."

Christopher smiled, gave Tim a hug, and listened to his news. But he was very grave with me. A little later, when the boys were out of earshot, he lowered his voice and said, "Sweetheart, you shouldn't have told Timothy. You've got his hopes up, but what if nothing happens? Believe what you want to believe, but don't mess with Tim's mind. If nothing happens it would be too cruel for words."

Of course, on one level he's quite right. It would be cruel, too awful to contemplate. But I don't have to contemplate it, do I? I mean, Jesus promised me, direct to my heart, and what's more, it's in His Word. And if it says so, then it is so (yes, I'm becoming an expert now)!

We've been lied to all this time; it's not just spiritual healing being promised in Isaiah 53:5. Gloria Copeland says... ah, I'm getting ahead of myself.

You see, it was the *Believers' Voice of Victory* that I'd been watching. At the end of the program they offered a gift for Mother's Day.

I phoned to get it, and the person on the other end of the line offered to pray with me. I told them what had happened, and it turns out that they have a story of a boy called Desmond Oomen from Holland, who was healed of autism.

Can you believe it! They sent me the magazine featuring the story, as well as a CD interview with the family.

We all sat on Christopher's bed and watched it together on his computer. Tim was bouncing up and down and hugging me. I can't tell you how lovely it was to see him so happy, so full of hope.

Christopher was smiling at Tim's enthusiasm. "That's great, big son, that's great." But to me, he said, "Well, you know what I think. I just hope you're right."

Anyway, I've bought a series of teachings from Gloria Copeland called "Healing School." It's brilliant, and I'm learning so much. Although I only manage about five minutes at a time because I keep falling asleep. Oh dear, I really have to concentrate so hard to understand what she's saying!

I'm taking notes to try to stay awake, but still, one minute I'm listening and half an hour later I wake up with dribble on my notepad!

I did hope that James would be sleeping better. But not yet…

Dear Mary,

We finally received Tim's report from the neuro-psychologist. Before I even started to read it, I mentally wrote SUBJECT TO CHANGE in red across the whole thing. I prayed and read scriptures to encourage myself, and then I read it.

She noted: "His behavior during the assessment suggested significant problems with executive/frontal function, poor understanding of complex language, and he presented as highly anxious.

"Timothy's perceptual motor problems cause him to struggle translating the visual image into the movements to copy it.

"Testing reveals that he has severe executive problems, and in everyday life, his difficulties become much more obvious. His difficulties with problem solving, task initiation, organization, and flexible thinking are exacerbated by his extreme anxiety and his underlying language and perceptual problems. He also has great difficulties with self-regulation, and he experiences mood shifts and extreme emotions.

"Given the severity of his executive and emotional problems, Timothy would be unable to function in a mainstream class, even with designated on-to-one supervision. He needs a specialist educational setting that would provide much more structure, routine, repetition, processing time, social support, and an emphasis on multi-sensory teaching and learning."

I sat back, gulped down some chamomile tea, and prayed awhile.

In a couple of short paragraphs, she'd summarized a myriad of problems we'd faced every day of Tim's life.

While his struggles and our observations were validated, it was still quite a blow to see it there in black and white.

Thank the Lord for tea! Another cup while declaring, "Thank You, Lord, that Tim is healed. Thank You, Lord, that every part of him functions the way You created it to function. Thank You, Lord, that greater is He that is in Tim than he that is in the world.

"Thank You, Lord, that You are greater than autism, dysexecutive syndrome, anxiety, depression, and everything else! Thank You, Lord, that Tim has been redeemed from the curse and is blessed. I am so grateful, Father, that You have healed him."

Dear Mary,

But the report carried on: "There are significant problems with emotional function, communication skills, and executive skills, meaning Timothy has difficulty applying his ability to academic tasks and everyday life.

"In my opinion, although some form of autistic spectrum disorder may be a component of his complex developmental difficulties, this of itself is not a sufficient explanation for these findings. Timothy has impaired ability to retrieve visual or spoken information from permanent memory."

I'd always known that Timothy was intelligent, which was why his inability to retain what he'd learned had baffled me so much. He learned, but afterwards, he couldn't access or keep that information. No wonder he was so discouraged.

"There is a specific and significant delay in the development of number skills and numerical understanding. His perceptual deficit also results in perceptual motor problems that make for handwritten and recording difficulties in written words and math."

Such simple words, and yet behind them were years of struggling, frustration, and distress, as Tim had tried to cope with basic writing and learning.

A few more gulps of tea while I remembered, with awful guilt, the times I'd become angry and frustrated with him.

"Oh Tim, I'm so sorry," I whispered. "I'm so sorry." Oh, the guilt. I should have done better. My best was simply not good enough. "Oh Lord, I'm so sorry, help me. Please make it up to him."

And the report went on: "Another major component of Timothy's neuro-developmental profile is impaired executive/frontal function. In Timothy's case, his executive problems affect his mood states, adaptive function, and self-regulation, as well as neural sensitivity to a range of stimuli.

"Timothy has difficulty regulating his moods and anxiety levels. In unfamiliar or stressful circumstances, he quickly becomes hyper-aroused and experiences overpowering anxiety that results in outbursts that resemble panic attacks. Timothy tries to use cognitive strategies to control his panic and hyper-arousal, but this is very fatiguing, and he is unable to sustain it for long."

His "difficulty regulating his emotions" seemed benign in print, but her simple words brought back a myriad of memories.

"Difficulty regulating moods and anxiety levels" didn't begin to describe the storms of emotions that he and the whole family had dealt with for years.

"Timothy's frontal problems coexist with difficulties with social and communication skills." His difficulties were mainly with pragmatic/semantic processing that is closely linked to frontal and right hemisphere function. "He experiences debilitating levels of anxiety, and this is often manifest in rocking and stereotype or rigid and uncompromising behaviors.

"He is neither educationally, emotionally, or socially equipped to cope in a mainstream school. To put him in this situation could precipitate a complete mental breakdown."

Well, that was pretty clear. She went on to privately suggest to me that Timothy exhibited significant signs of Bipolar Disorder. His mood swings were getting worse, and he should be on stabilizing medication, which he would most likely need to take for life.

He suffered times of deep depression during which he didn't feel that life was worth living. Having spent a significant amount of time with him, and through reading some of his poetry, she stated that she believed he was at high risk of suicide.

More tea and then some more. But you know what, I'm not sure exactly when, but I seem to have swapped the whisky for drinking this tea, and I think that has to be a good thing.

Dear Mary,

Thank You, Lord, that my children are taught by You, and great is their peace (Isa. 54:13). Thank You, Lord, that Tim's mind, senses, and emotions are all healed and function perfectly.

I will not be moved (Ps. 125:1). I will not be afraid (Isa. 41:10). God is good, His Word is true, and all is well. Speaking in tongues and tea—the perfect way to keep calm! (Jude 1:20)

Thank You, Lord, that Tim's body is healed. Every nerve, muscle, and joint functions perfectly, as You designed them to function. I forbid any malfunction in his body, in Jesus' name.

What can I say? I'm just so grateful and relieved that we received the report after God gave me a revelation about healing.

Because I was able to read it all through the eyes of hope and not despair.

CHAPTER 18

Dear Mary,

It's been awhile, and I've so much to tell you. The boys are getting better. Yes, it's true. It's not just wishful thinking, they really are.

We had an appointment to see a specialist psychiatrist at Great Ormond Street Hospital, with regards to Tim and bipolar.

But after that night where Jesus promised to heal the boys, I wasn't sure if I should go or not. I was praying about it for days.

Then I sat with the phone in my hand and asked, "OK Lord, do I cancel, or do we go?" I hardly breathed, because I so badly wanted to hear Him. And He said loud and clear in my heart, *"Timothy and James will never need a psychiatrist."*

I screamed and threw the phone down. I ran shouting up and down the sitting room, "They'll never need a psychiatrist, they'll never need a psychiatrist!"

"Tim, Tim, you'll never need a psychiatrist. God said you'll never need a psychiatrist!"

We were dancing around laughing. I grabbed the phone. "I'm cancelling the appointment Tim, you know why?"

And he said, "Because I'll never need a psychiatrist!" Too right! So, I cancelled, and it felt so good to say, "We don't need the appointment, thank you."

Tim hasn't had unstable moods now for some time. He's been absolutely fine all these months. Isn't that great? Isn't that brilliant? I'm so happy!

Timothy and James will never need a psychiatrist!

Dear Mary,

Oh, I have to tell you about our little Jamie. The other day, Bob from next door gave us a cucumber from his greenhouse.

James and Khloe (Yes, he has made friends with the little girl across the road!) broke it in half and munched the whole thing up!

He ate it just like that! You could have knocked me down with a feather! He eats raw green beans and carrots. He eats little blocks of cheese, and chicken, and dry cereal, and bread.

He loves chips and potato waffles. It's wonderful. We have joined a home education group. He loves to look at the other children; he watches them play, and just laughs and laughs. He thinks their antics are hilarious!

He used to refuse to go into the park if other children were there, but now he goes in tentatively, and spends ages watching them, intrigued.

The other day Khloe was off school, poorly. Her mum left her with us while she went to work. I prayed over her, and a short while later they were both playing in the garden, happy as can be!

He'll be four soon; my baby's growing up! He's still not speaking—well, not English anyway. He talks his own language with gestures. Tim and I can usually understand him. Khloe, bless her little heart, sometimes looks a bit perplexed, but I'm always there to interpret.

He's connecting with us now, and he's really starting to notice the world around him. The best way to explain it is that it's like he's slowly waking up.

I'm so glad I refused to make him learn PECS. I just know he'll talk.

I love Charles Capps's booklet *"God's Creative Power for Healing"* and speak the confessions out loud whenever I have a moment. I just keep it in my pocket and reach for it whenever I can.

I also play healing scripture CDs in the hallway while we're sleeping, and in the kitchen when I'm getting on with stuff. It builds up my faith and keeps me encouraged.

James's nights are still pretty bad, but I know they'll get better, which makes it easier to bear.

I'm trusting God. This is a much happier household now; there's a different atmosphere. It's amazing what hope can do!

Dear Mary,

It's almost Christmas. The sweetest thing happened the other day. I have some mistletoe hanging up in the sitting room doorway. When Christopher or Timothy are nearby, I sneak quick kisses in.

Tim laughs and makes a big thing about trying to escape my clutches. Christopher grabs me and makes big growly, snoggy noises, to which Tim responds with great disgust!

But I know better than to try to kiss our little Jamie. Although he's improving in some ways, he still shies away from physical contact and appears to be in his own world, unaware of what's going on around him a lot of the time.

But without us realizing it, he had obviously been taking this little scenario in, because one day I came around the corner, and there he was on a little stool, which he had pulled up under the mistletoe, and he ambushed me with a full-on, face-smashing kiss!

Oh, I can't describe the joy! My first Jamie kiss. It had taken four years of loving, loving, loving and giving more than I thought I had to give, and he's finally responding.

It was quite painful. He wrapped his little arms around my neck and practically head butted me! But it was my first hug and kiss! The best Christmas present ever. Our very own Christmas miracle!

It's just the four of us again. I find Christmases really hard. We make a big thing of decorating the tree and playing carols. (James loves the *Tijuana Christmas* CD. He used to put his hands over his ears and shout if we put music on, but now he's dancing around to it.)

But it's usually just us. No family, no friends. Christopher's parents were here last year. So, it will probably be another two or three years before they join us for Christmas again.

My family doesn't bother to visit anymore. They have all their own special traditions, and we're not part of them. In some ways it's probably just as well, really, but I do wish we weren't so alone, year after year.

Dear Mary,

Yay, summer is here, and we're getting out of the house! We went for a walk in the woods last week with the home education group, and the boys had a great time.

We're off to the park tomorrow. I've met a woman with a little girl about James's age. The little girl has Asperger's, but she and James seemed to be companionable in the park. They're coming around to visit us next week. Phew, a veritable social whirl!

Tim's been going ice skating with some of the children from our home education group and is enjoying it so much. James and I just toddle about together on the ice! He doesn't even seem to notice the loud music!

You know I was trying to get a Statement for Tim? Well anyway, when the LEA refused to assess him, I called them up. They said that we could appeal, but that it would then have to go to tribunal, and that we'd lose because Tim had never been to school.

So, I said that I had a sympathetic benefactor who had put unlimited funds at my disposal (God, obviously), and that I would fight to get that Statement. When I had prayed about this, I felt it was OK to pursue the Statement, so I also presumed God would provide the means.

I said we didn't have time to mess with tribunals, and I was going to employ my own private lawyers immediately, as I felt the LEA was breaking the law by insisting Timothy go to mainstream school against the advice of specialists.

We found a law firm in Wales, which specializes in educational law, and sent them all our information. They responded that we did indeed have a case, but that it would cost us £200 per hour.

The first thing to do would be to put together a letter with supporting reports. That would be five hours work.

They would begin as soon as we had paid the first £1 000. I just laughed and said, "God, You heard that. I believe You want us to go ahead with this, so I'm expecting You to give us the funds, thanks so much."

That was a Friday. On Sunday night, a friend of my mother offered us the first £1 000 to go legal! Funny enough, this chap was inclined to think I was an overprotective, rather neurotic mother. He seemed somewhat surprised at his own offer!

The letter was submitted with a cover letter from me, stating their legal responsibilities, my knowledge of the legal situation, and determination to pursue this until I was satisfied with their response.

Within a couple of weeks, the LEA had agreed to a Statement for Timothy, and what's more, they required no further assessments, as the reports we had submitted were now deemed to be sufficient!

No tribunal, no need to attend school or anymore assessments, no more time wasted, and not one penny more than the original £1,000 spent.

I realized that when God is on your side, and you are depending on Him to come through, stuff really does happen!

Then it dawned on me: This is how it is in the spiritual realm. Healing is our right, as believers, but that doesn't mean it's automatic. There is an enemy trying to deceive us into tolerating his agenda.

We need to stand up and insist on our rights! And if God is for us, who can stand against us (Rom. 8:31)?

Phew! Well, I am up for the fight!

Dear Mary,

We now have a detailed and comprehensive Statement and are being offered educational options for Timothy.

We had originally asked for funding so he could attend a private school. However, instead of allowing Timothy into this school (the Park House School in Peterborough, which specializes in ASD, or Autism Spectrum Disorder), I've been given a list of three other special schools in our vicinity. I need to visit them, decide which one is suitable, and report back to the authorities.

The first school is in "special measures," meaning that, as a result of severe failure, the leadership has been removed, and an emergency temporary team has been sent in to run it. I haven't even bothered to make an appointment with this one.

The second school is ghastly. Realizing that I was less than impressed, the teacher showing me around threw her hands in the air and said, "We wouldn't have taken your son anyway. Every child in this school has a sub-normal IQ, and he is in the normal range." So much for that one.

The third school was much the same as the second. As I was touring it with the head teacher, a large boy pushed past me, literally trying to escape. The whole place was locked up like a prison! Several staff members bolted after the child, tackled him, restrained him, and took him back inside while he wept, bellowing in despair.

It was extremely distressing. Afterwards, I sat in the car and cried for those children and their parents. Hell would freeze over before either of my boys went there.

I compiled my reports and submitted them. The LEA responded by suggesting a few more schools of the same ilk, spreading the net a little further afield to include schools not in our area.

I felt that they were wasting our time. Having learned how the system worked, I knew they'd send me to every special school in the country rather than fund Timothy's placement in a private specialist school.

I realized that even with the Statement, they had no intention of putting Timothy into the school I'd requested. By having me chase all over the country visiting other places and submitting more reports, they could keep us tied up far into the future, with Timothy getting no help in the meantime.

So, I have compiled a very strong letter, insisting they offer something more suitable to Timothy's needs, and threatening to go legal again if they don't.

So, we will see….

Dear Mary,

Well, the LEA has offered to fund Timothy a place at The Red Balloon in Cambridge. It's mainly a type of rehabilitation "school" for children who have been severely bullied or have other issues resulting in them being unable to attend mainstream education.

It's in a house in the city, and is very small, informal, and relaxed with no set curriculum. Tim likes it. Christopher and I aren't so sure, but having prayed about it, I have peace.

It's clear to me that as kind as the staff is, no one is trained to know how to deal with ASD, nor does anyone have a real understanding of the sensory issues Tim has. Unless God intervenes and sorts Tim out, he'll never be able to cope with it. But it really seems to me that God is saying Tim can go.

I'm not quite sure how to proceed. Do we wait until Tim is healed and then try to find something, fight for the specialist ASD school, or let him go to Red Balloon?

Thank goodness for tongues! I've been praying constantly, and we've decided to accept the place for Tim in Cambridge.

They arranged a taxi to transport him there and back daily. Just for two hours, 10 a.m. to 12 p.m. But after a few days, Tim simply couldn't cope and had to stop.

I didn't panic, and knowing that God was at work in the situation gave me peace. If he went back to the school, that was fine. If he didn't, that was fine as well, as long as we are being led in the right direction.

Anyway, I keep praying, and just hope that I am being led by God! If I make a mistake, I know He's big enough to fix it!

Dear Mary,

We had a meeting with the teachers to discuss some issues that Tim had. He is 12 years old now! Can you believe that? My lovely big boy will soon be a teenager.

Anyway, there have been some issues, so the school is implementing strategies to help, and Tim will go back in a few days.

I really believe he's meant to go back. So, I can only presume that there is some serious healing going on in him!

I discussed the situation with his neuro-psychologist. She was horrified that Tim was attending the school.

"Remove him immediately," she said. "He won't be able to function in that environment. They won't be able to identify, let alone ameliorate, the causes of his distress. In my opinion, to place such a mentally and emotionally vulnerable child in that environment constitutes child abuse!"

She advised me on what to put in my report to the LEA about why he shouldn't be there. She told me to stick to my guns with regards to the specialist school in Peterborough.

However, she emphasized that in her professional opinion, the only place where Timothy would be able to function to his full potential was a specialized boarding school for children with autism. She believes that we have enough evidence to insist that the LEA fund a place for him there.

I know she's right, in the natural, that is. Everything she says makes sense. We've even found a school that might be suitable and have looked at the options of moving (again) so that we could be close to it, allowing Timothy to become a weekly boarder while coming home on weekends.

I've been in contact with the school, and I had all their literature. This advice has come from the highest authority in the country, so I trust her more than anyone else we've encountered.

And yet... every time I pray, I feel peace about sending him back to Red Balloon.

Dear Mary,

I've been praying in tongues 'round the clock, while getting on with everything else, and reading scriptures to encourage myself.

James 1:5—If any of you lacks wisdom, let him ask of God, who gives to all liberally and without reproach, and it will be given to him.

John 10:4—And when he brings out his own sheep, he goes before them; and the sheep follow him, for they know his voice.

On Monday, Tim was ready to go back. I knew it would challenge him in so many ways, and that unless we had a miracle, he would not cope, just as the neuropsychologist anticipates.

But he's gone. As he waved me goodbye this morning, pale little face, smiling nervously, my stomach lurched with anxiety.

"Oh Lord, keep him safe. I'm trusting You. He's in Your hands. Thank You that he's healed. Thank You that You have good plans for him. Thank You that he's well able to cope. Thank You that he's blessed and not cursed. Thank You that he'll fulfill Your plans for his life. Thank You that the plans of the enemy come to nothing. In Jesus' name."

I refused to allow myself to cry or worry. I felt butterflies in my stomach. "There is no fear in love," I said (1 John 4:18); "God has not given [me] a spirit of fear" (2 Tim. 1:7).

I spent that morning reading scriptures and declaring that Tim was free to be the person God created him to be.

When he arrived home, I was waiting at the window, James on my hip. The moment he saw me, he smiled and waved, running happily into the house. "I've had a great day," he grinned cheerfully, giving me a big hug. "It was good."

Yes, it was good. God is good, and His Word is true. I knew a miracle had taken place that day. He's getting better and better day by day; he was being set free.

Although the specialists had been right in the natural, they had not been able to take the power of God and His Word into the equation.

But we had, and miracles were starting to unfold before our very eyes!

CHAPTER 18

Dear Mary,

This is what the National Autistic Society says about autism: "Autism is a lifelong developmental disability that affects how people perceive the world and interact with others. Autistic people see, hear and feel the world differently to other people. If you are autistic, you are autistic for life; autism is not an illness or disease and cannot be 'cured.' It is a fundamental aspect of their identity."

And this, Mary, is what I'm trying to get my head around. In the natural, this explanation/definition is perfectly reasonable. But I'm challenging it because I'm coming at it from a spiritual aspect.

Being in the world, but no longer of the world (John 17:14), means that these natural rules and laws no longer apply with regard to disabilities.

We are in the kingdom of God now and have access to the supernatural, where spiritual laws dominate the natural. In the spiritual, healing has been made available to us through Jesus and His death on the cross (1 Peter 2:24).

My children have a blood-bought right to be completely healed!

I was praying the other day, "Lord, it's so hard to walk in faith ('walk by faith and not by sight'—2 Cor. 5:7) when the symptoms of autism are in front of my face every day."

While I was praying, I saw a picture of a screen in my mind's eye; a plain, white screen. Then there were images of blood, death, and horror flashing across it. *"The screen is still perfect,"* the Lord said. *"Those images are on the screen, but they aren't an integral part of the screen.*

"Autism is a projection on to your children. I created them to be perfect; it's not an integral part of who they are. That is the lie."

Then the plug was pulled, the images flickered and faded away, leaving a perfect, clear screen. *"You need to pull the plug."*

Pull the plug! Just pull the plug on autism! Sounds so easy, but how? How do I do that, Lord?

He showed me that there were three ways that autism was empowered to remain entrenched:

Fear it. Believe it. Speak it. We've been deceived into using our own God-given authority to establish and empower this evil projection of autism. We have the power to establish it, or to pull the plug and banish it!

I scribbled those three things onto a piece of paper: *Don't fear autism, don't believe autism, don't speak autism.* I have asked the Holy Spirit to help me, and to remind me of this in everyday life.

I will not fear autism. I will not be intimidated, impressed, or disheartened by the symptoms I see. I diminish them and magnify God and His promises.

I will not believe that any of these symptoms or characteristics are an integral part of my children. I recognize that they are a projection of the enemy, and they have no power to stay anymore, because I have found out the deception! I am no longer deceived into believing it.

I will not speak autism. I will not call my children autistic. They are healed. They are perfect. Autism is external to them, an illegitimate imposition of the enemy. I will not empower it by the words of my mouth. And it cannot stay!

Once I got the picture that, as a born-again believer, I was more powerful than autism, it completely lost its power over me (Luke 10:19).

It simply could not distress or worry me anymore. It was history. It was past tense!

Any show of "strength" through symptoms or behaviors was simply a desperate attempt to frighten and intimidate me into believing the lie. It won't work anymore. I have become 100% convinced that it's fading like a projection on a screen with the plug pulled out.

I am thrilled, delighted, and I am empowered!

Dear Mary,

I'm watching my words so carefully now. I'm amazed at how many dreadful things I used to say without even realizing it!

I've been telling Timothy about it, and now he's absolutely ruthless about correcting me when I slip up!

Sometimes it's so irritating! I have to grit my teeth and say the right thing, when I just want to have a good old rant!

I get so tired of trying to change my thoughts and my words, I just want to relax, take a break, and say what I feel. I want to tell Christopher what a hard day I've had. I want some acknowledgement of my selfless suffering! I want some sympathy, some pity!

I want someone to acknowledge what a martyr I've been. How sad and pathetic I am! I've learned when I get in that sort of mood, to start praising God. To sing to Him, to thank Him for everything I can think of, and to sing in tongues. Soon I get over myself and feel encouraged again.

To think that the sympathy and pity I sometimes want is like poison to my children, to think that it will sabotage God's healing power in their lives—that is a very sobering thought indeed.

And now, whenever I start thinking like this, I see Joyce Meyer and her wind-up robot: "What about me? What about me? Beep, beep. What about me?"

The Holy Spirit has a sense of humor!

Dear Mary,

I know this is weird, but bear with me while I try to explain. I feel like there are two me's. And whichever one gets fed, it takes over.

I decided, nearly two years ago now, that I wouldn't watch anymore TV or movies, read any more books or magazines—other than good Christian teaching—until our boys were completely healed.

But sometimes I just want to watch something simple and entertaining. I'm tired of reading the Bible, and I'm fed up with all this "holy" stuff.

I'm tired of watching and challenging my thoughts and words.

Oh Lord, I'm so sorry, I don't think I'm a very good person. I just want to watch Poirot, eat chocolate, have a big glass of wine, and perhaps have a little moan!

Sigh. What's more, I realize that each of those things is not bad in itself (except the moaning!), but I'm too vulnerable and new to this spiritual stuff to get away with feeding the wrong self (although both of us are having the chocolate).

I know that sounds really odd. How can I explain it?

So the other day, Christopher and I were chatting about how to spend more time together. I always go to bed at the same time as James.

We decided that one evening a week, I'd stay up and spend an hour or so with Christopher. But we had nothing much to say to each other! Once he'd said a bit about work, and I'd given an update on the boys, we ran out of conversation!

So, we thought we'd get a movie and watch that together, snuggled up on the sofa. We watched *Sleepless in Seattle,* holding hands, cuddling. Apart from my drifting off a couple of times, it was lovely.

Then we went to bed—he to his room, and me to mine—creeping in so as not to wake Jamie. But do you think I could sleep?

No way! Panic hit me so hard I could barely breathe. What if I was wrong? What if I hadn't really heard God? What if I was really ruining my boys' lives?

What if they never got healed? I'd stopped all their therapies. Was I stark raving mad?

What if *I* was mentally ill and didn't realize it? What if there really wasn't a God after all? My heart was thumping, and I broke out in a sweat.

Oh God, help me, what if I'm talking to myself, mad as a hatter? The Christians think I'm a radical fanatic, the non-Christians just laugh and think I'm odd, the medical lot think I'm ruining my children's lives and that I'm irresponsible and un-cooperative.

And I think I'm right. But what if I'm wrong and everyone else is right?

Then James started wrestling with his duvet, grinding his teeth, and making growling noises of fury.

Oh my God! Look at that child! How did I think things were OK? Nothing's OK! It's all bad, bad, bad!

What am I doing? What am I going to do? I was absolutely terrified, frozen in horror.

Like an automaton, I settled James, and soothed him back to sleep. But I lay there shivering with shock and fear, trying to think clearly through the panic.

I didn't want to pray, because suddenly I wasn't sure I'd be heard. I couldn't remember any scriptures except the Lord's Prayer, so I started saying it in my head, wondering if I was actually deranged.

Then I remembered 2 Timothy 1:7— "For God has not given us a spirit of fear, but of power and of love and of a sound mind."

Then I remembered the *Amplified* version: "For God did not give us a spirit of timidity (of cowardice, of craven and cringing and fawning fear), but [He has given us a spirit] of power and of love and of calm and well-balanced mind and discipline and self-control" (AMPC).

Then I said Colossians 3:2-3 out loud, "And set your minds and keep them set on what is above (the higher things), not on the things that are on the earth. For [as far as this world is concerned] you have died, and your [new, real] life is hidden with Christ in God" (AMPC).

Dear Mary,

It took me three days, three whole days, to get myself in a safe, calm, secure place again!

I've heard some preachers talk about a "flesh flash." Well, I've lived my whole life just occasionally having a "spirit flash!"

I simply can't afford to start thinking the old way. I am too new to this renewing of my mind (Eph. 4:23) and to thinking God's way.

I'm too vulnerable to fall back into the old ways of thinking, because when I do, I go to pieces!

Anyway, that was the end of our date nights! I was so exhausted the next day. And I was more determined than ever not to watch anything worldly at all! Christopher was disappointed, but shrugged and said, "That's OK, my darling, we'll get there eventually." He's so lovely.

Now I'm feeding my spiritual self like crazy and starving my worldly self as best I can.

However, what a sobering experience it was. It wasn't funny at all. I'm realizing more and more what the Bible means about the enemy coming to steal, kill, and destroy, and roaming around like a roaring lion seeking whom he may devour (John 10:10; 1 Peter 5:8).

Well, I don't intend to be devoured, nor let my children be. I'm going for the life in abundance till it overflows a bit, thank You, Jesus.

Galatians 6:7-8— "Do not be deceived and deluded and misled; God will not allow Himself to be sneered at (scorned, disdained, or mocked by mere pretensions or professions, or by His precepts being set aside.) [He inevitably deludes himself who attempts to delude God.] For whatever a man sows, that and that only is what he will reap. For he who sows to his own flesh (lower nature, sensuality) will from the flesh reap decay and ruin and destruction, but he who sows to the Spirit will from the Spirit reap eternal life" (AMPC).

I have been shaken to my core, and I'm now more serious and determined than ever before to believe and walk in the Spirit.

CHAPTER 20

Dear Mary,

It's spring 2008. The little lambs are in the fields with their mothers. The butterflies and bumblebees are busy in the hedgerows. And the trees, naked only a couple of weeks ago, are clothed in lush green. England at this time of year is beautiful.

Yesterday we headed off to a big park nearby for a picnic with the home education group.

Yes, we do things like that these days! There was Jamie, sitting on the picnic rug, munching happily on green beans and a cucumber, wearing normal clothes, and staring at the other children as though he'd never seen them before.

In many ways, he hadn't. He's been confined in his own private world for so much of his life.

In the past, if there'd been more than one or two other people in the park, he'd refused to enter. Now, as he watched the children play, it seemed he was taking it all in.

After lunch, he wandered over and played alongside the other children. I watched as he walked up to strangers and initiated little conversations. They couldn't understand him but tried to be polite. All the while, I held my breath and almost danced for joy. My James is creeping out of his world and starting to interact with people!

All these firsts are so exciting and encouraging, and Tim is also improving—no more extreme mood swings, and he's actually coping with and enjoying his "school."

I was chatting to another mum in the park while our children played (oh, how good it is to be able to say that!).

She has a little girl, a year younger than James, who has been diagnosed with Asperger's Syndrome. Because James has improved so much, I invited them over for a visit.

We'll see how that goes.

Dear Mary,

Well, they have been visiting weekly for a few months now. Christopher is so happy for me. He is delighted that I finally have a friend and that James is playing with another child. He pleads with me to be polite and not so forthright and outspoken. He knows that I can offend English people with my South African straight talk.

However, it's getting very difficult to restrain myself. You see, I've gone through all that palaver of releasing unforgiveness and bitterness. I've learned not to rehearse injustices and unkind behavior of people, but simply to give it to God, and let it go.

God has really emphasized the need to walk in forgiveness. So, when this woman goes on and on about her in-laws and issues with family due to her daughter's problems, I can relate, but I don't want to go there. I understand why she feels so hurt and misunderstood; I've been there myself, but I simply don't want to talk these things over and over.

I told her about how God healed my heart and changed my attitude. But it didn't seem to have much impact on her.

At times I've been so tempted to tell her my own horror stories, but I can't afford to fall into that trap, so I keep trying to change the subject, being sensitive to her feelings, while guarding my own words.

Because she's a Spirit-filled Methodist, I thought she'd understand when I told her all about how God had promised to heal the boys and all that I'd learned about healing being provided at the cross. But although she seemed pleased, she by no means grasped the concept.

She didn't seem to really believe me when I told her about how much James had improved. She keeps pointing out his obvious problems. She notes every lingering symptom and suggests intervention strategies and homeopathic remedies.

Now, Christopher, Tim, and I are so careful not to talk about the problems, but only to speak God's truth about them, so I told her, "We believe that James is healed."

This fell on deaf ears because it was as though she felt she had to show me how wrong I was by highlighting any issues she saw.

As a trained school teacher, she pointed out James's developmental delay, his behavioral problems, and then she prescribed what I should do about them. Explaining that her daughter could already read and write, she handed me some teaching materials, saying, "You should teach James."

Biting my tongue, I took the materials. I knew she was trying to be helpful, despite having so many challenges of her own.

In many ways, I feel sorry for her. She is trying so hard, while I'm floating around in a bubble of joy and relief. I know that I can't fix my children. I also know that God is at work doing what most people consider impossible. So, I just shut up and try to ignore and overlook all her comments.

She takes her daughter to a Christian homeopath and keeps a constant watch over her, carrying a box of remedies around to treat every issue that arises, including the child's mood regulation. She told me, "My daughter is on a grain-, gluten- and dairy-free diet," and then she goes off talking about the problems she sees in

James's diet. Every time I say, "He's fine," she explains why he's not. It's exasperating.

I'm trusting in God and His promises in the Word, and her faith is in her homeopath and remedies. I wouldn't trade places with her for the world! But my patience is running thin. I'm not enjoying this, but I don't want to sabotage James's chance to have a little friend.

Dear Mary,

Oh no! What on earth? She has just told me, "I've given your names to our prayer chain." When I looked surprised, she went on to explain how it works: A bunch of people we don't know are suddenly speaking our names in prayer.

What do these people believe? What sorts of things do they pray for? I know enough to realize that most Christians don't even believe in healing, especially something like autism.

Nor do many of them genuinely believe the Bible. I don't want them praying for my boys! Who knows what stories are being passed on, like "churchified" Chinese whispers and spiritualized gossip? I want it to stop.

Then the last straw: "I chatted with my homeopath about James, and he said…." But I was too angry to listen anymore. After I'd explained our spiritual stand, I heard her nattering on about James's brain working incorrectly, about hormones and remedies. I cut her short.

"I couldn't care less about what the homeopath or anyone else says, I'm not taking him to any doctor, homeopath, or specialist ever again!" She looked hurt and offended.

This is not working. We do not need this anymore.

On top of this, even though she's constantly complaining about her in-laws, her own family seems really supportive and helpful, often spending weeks at a time with her. They're even selling their home to move closer, to help her more regularly.

So now I find myself dwelling on how our families have rejected us, as we receive absolutely no help from them at all. I start feeling sorry for myself again, even though I know self-pity is poison to faith.

I find myself feeling resentful and upset. Then I realize I need to get my emotions under control.

I'm going to have to stop these visits, as this is a relationship I cannot afford to have.

CHAPTER 21

Dear Mary,

God is good, and all is well. I keep saying that. I have to hold on to it—to walk by faith and not by sight.

My word, it's hard. We're having problems here, but I won't give in. I won't give up. My boys are healed, and nothing in the physical will convince me otherwise. But we're having a hard time.

I can hardly bear to even say it... James has regressed! I know I shouldn't cry, I'm trying to stand in faith, but I'm deeply disappointed, and so exhausted, and I just can't believe what's happened.

The day after his fifth birthday, James started insisting we close the curtains because the light was bothering him. Then he started putting his hands over his ears again. He won't eat anything but pureed oatmeal now, which I have to feed him, and he's getting so thin.

He won't leave the house or let me out of his sight. He freaks out if anyone visits. It's horrendous. Our whole world has shrunk down again. No music, no light, just Thomas the Tank Engine over and over and over again.

He hates eye contact and shouts, "No look me," if he sees us looking at him. He's become quite aggressive. He smashes his train tracks up, then wants me to build them again, then smashes them up again, over and over....

Poor Timothy. James has it in for him. He hates me giving any attention to Tim. Actually, he even tries to stop me from hugging Christopher. He tries to push us apart, shouting, "No, no!"

He's become utterly contrary. He does the opposite of what he thinks we want him to do.

Oh, my goodness, Mary, I've got to remind myself, *don't fear autism, don't believe autism, don't speak autism.*

But he was doing so well, and I'm gutted. I should have shut her up and refuted her words, as it says in Isaiah 54:17, "No weapon formed against you shall prosper, and every tongue which rises against you in judgment you shall condemn."

I know her motives were good, but in her ignorance of how God's kingdom works, she has spoken. And in my desire to be polite and not offend anybody, I kept quiet.

I should have condemned those words. It seems like such a little thing, yet the repercussions are huge. The enemy used that situation. Autism has been empowered, and James has suffered a terrible regression.

Well, I've learned a lesson. I will not give up. Tim and James are healed, and I will not tolerate anything else. I will keep on believing.

I will see my boys set perfectly free.

Dear Mary,

Well, it's Christmas time again, and 2008 is coming to an end. The tree is up, the lights and decorations sparkling cheerfully, the mistletoe in its usual place. What a difference a year makes. Last year I had my first Jamie kiss. This year he's completely withdrawn, quiet, thin, and only interested in his trains.

Christopher ran a half-marathon recently (the Great North Run between Newcastle upon Tyne and South Shields) with a whole bunch of people from work. He trained for months to do it. He says that the running really helps keep him mentally up and positive.

He's also been working long hours in preparation for his company's annual Christmas conference. The day after which he came home and went to bed.

And that was it. He just collapsed like a popped balloon. After a week of complete exhaustion, I managed to coax him to see a doctor.

"I've seen this in businessmen before," the doctor said. "Sometimes they push themselves too far for too long until they just break. Christopher, you really should take a year off; you're suffering from burnout."

Now Tim's fallen ill. Back to the doctor, where this time he diagnosed glandular fever.

So, they're both in bed, and the house is very quiet. I can't let this oppressive atmosphere stay. I keep speaking healing scriptures over us all, and I keep making up little songs and singing them over and over to encourage myself: "This will be our best Christmas yet, we are all strong and we are healthy."

But the nights are hell. As long as we stick to the routine, James goes to sleep fine, but about half an hour later, it starts. He grinds his teeth and makes loud growly, rage-like noises. He shouts out, either really angry or absolutely terrified. He flings himself all over the place like he's wrestling something, eyes wide open but somehow unseeing.

If I manage to wake him up, he sobs and sobs inconsolably. He head-butts the wall... and me. I wake up sometimes to him raining blows all over me. He's five now and getting bigger. He's really able to hurt me. It's awful. But he never remembers anything after he's woken up.

The other night I woke to him hitting me while he kicked and kicked. Not fully awake, I snapped. Before I realized what I was doing, I'd swung around and punched as hard as I could.

My fist smashed into the pillow right beside his face. I'll never forget the horror of that moment.

Later, after James was asleep again, I lay in the darkness with my heart pounding in my chest. "Lord," I whispered, "what on earth am I to do? What has happened to my family?"

Everything seemed to be going wrong. Now Christopher is shattered. Timothy's glands are still swollen, and he is so unwell. And James...

But I'm not giving in. I'm not going to feel sorry for myself, for us. I am a child of God.

I have His Word. He says that by Jesus' stripes we are healed (Isa. 53:5). If it says so, then it is so.

And that's final.

Dear Mary,

Well, something quite funny happened last night. When Christopher and the boys were asleep, I was pacing up and down the sitting room, declaring God's Word over our situation: "We are victorious, and not victims. We are healed and not sick. We are rich and not poor. The Word says it, My God has promised it, and I'm having it. I will settle for nothing less."

Then I'd speak the scriptures and pray in tongues. Up and down the sitting room I went, till my legs buckled under me and I sank down on the sofa, exhausted. "Lord, I'm so tired. How can I carry on?"

Then I heard God in my heart, *"You have formidable energy."*

I had to laugh, sitting there in a collapsed heap of exhaustion on that sofa. But I knew the choice was mine, to receive it or reject it. I could either believe Him or believe what my body was feeling.

So, I said: "OK, if You say so, then it is so, and I'm having it!" And I jumped up and shouted in a whisper, "I have formidable energy, I have formidable energy."

I began to laugh. As I laughed, all the anxiety of our situation fell away, and I had absolute confidence that God was true to His Word, and we'd be alright.

I started speaking again, and this time there was more power. "I will not be moved by what I see! I will not be moved by how I feel. God's Word does not return to Him void!"

I spoke out Isaiah 40:28-31, Isaiah 46:11, Isaiah 55:11, Jeremiah 1:12, and Jeremiah 29:11. Then I grabbed my list of favorite healing scriptures and spoke them out with renewed fervency and strength.

Scriptures on prosperity, on protection, on guidance—I read them all, I spoke them, and I prayed in tongues.

Then I took myself off to bed, physically and emotionally refreshed, giggling like a carefree schoolgirl, knowing that if God is for us, no one could stand against us (Rom. 8:31).

Dear Mary,

Some days, I sit companionably with James, and while he watches DVDs, I seize the moment to do some reading.

I always have a pile of books on the go, grabbing any opportunity I can to read them.

I'm racing through *Protecting Your Families in Dangerous Times* by Kelly Copeland at the moment, which really helps build up my faith in God's protection. I have always loved Psalm 91. It gives me such peace, knowing we have guardian angels watching over us all.

While I've been learning about healing, I've also discovered that God wants us to be prosperous. I've been mulling over 3 John 2 recently and have decided that I may as well have faith in financial prosperity as well as healing.

I'm tired of struggling financially. I'm tired of seeing Christopher work himself into total exhaustion just to keep our heads above water. It's God's will to prosper us financially, and that's wonderful news to me.

Years ago, someone gave me a tract by George Watson called "Others may, you cannot!" which suggests that God sovereignly chooses some people for suffering in the form of poverty, illness, and failure to keep them humble and close to Him.

The person felt "led" to give it to me. Over the years, I've been so perplexed as to why God wants to make me struggle with illnesses and lack of money. Why would He keep punishing me, when in my heart of hearts, all I wanted was to please Him?

Now I have finally realized that the extreme sovereignty of God teaching is absolutely wrong (that tract was just wrong, wrong, wrong).

It's His will to heal and prosper us! I'm so excited and happy! I'm taking all of His promises at face value and running with them.

However, this is really the good news I wanted to share. I've been reading Deuteronomy 8:18, Psalm 1:3, Malachi 3:10, 2 Corinthians 9:8, and Philippians 4:19-20. Christopher and I don't go to a church (impossible with the boys), but we have been tithing (a tenth of) our income to a ministry for a couple of years.

God is really dealing with me about trusting Him in every part of my life. I don't have any money of my own, but God has started prompting me to give some of my stuff away, starting with my jewelry. I don't have very much, and I never wear any of it, because my lifestyle doesn't allow it right now. But I always hoped that someday I'd have the opportunity to wear it again.

My little amethyst ring, some silver earrings, a few other bits and bobs.... I've sorted them out and wrapped them up in the little mother-of-pearl inlaid wooden jewelry box Christopher bought for me from abroad.

Somebody came to mind, and I knew I should give it to her. God was working in my heart, asking me to trust Him. So, I did. I gave them away.

While feeding James a few days later, I realized I had quite a few duplicate books from various ministries, as well as some books I hadn't really been interested in finishing. And I felt God leading me to give them all to a couple who ran a home group nearby.

Packing everything in the car, I left to run my errand, happy to get out of the house. In the middle of an intersection, after turning on a green light, I looked up and gasped. A huge truck had barreled through a red light and was heading towards me at high speed.

Frightened, I turned hard, hitting a small island in the road, and stalled.

The last thing I saw was the horrified face of the passenger in the truck as it hurtled towards me. The next moment, I found myself on the side of the road, about three car lengths down. My car was in neutral and running. There had been no impact.

I sat there, dumbstruck with astonishment. A woman walked past the car, not even looking at me. A white van drove by. It was as though nothing had happened at all.

I sat there for a few minutes, gathering my wits, recalling the truck coming at me, just the way the truck had borne down on us when I was pregnant with Timothy. Back then, Christopher had escaped into the hedgerow. But this time, escape had been impossible. That's when I realized a miracle had just taken place.

Arriving back home later, I ran upstairs to tell Christopher and Tim (both still ill) about what had happened. Tim laughed and hugged me. Christopher held my hand and shook his head. "Oh my darling, oh, sweetheart…."

My heart was so full of love and gratitude. "Thank You, Lord, for protecting me. My family needs me. Thank You for keeping me safe."

CHAPTER 22

Dear Mary,

I keep singing, "The joy of the Lord is my strength, the Lord is the strength of my life, I can do all things through Christ who strengthens me." I'm still looking after these three 'round the clock, and things don't look too good right now. But I will not be discouraged; I am trusting God.

I keep reading scriptures and praying in tongues, but Romans 8:28 has been bothering me a bit. It says that "... all things work together for good to those who love God, to those who are the called according to His purpose."

Of course, I want all things to work together for good, even in this difficult circumstance. But for this scripture to apply to me, I have to be "called according to His purpose." What does that mean? I'm not sure.

I need to have the assurance that, despite the way things look, all things are working together for our good. But am I the called according to His purpose? I've been thinking about it a lot. And then I read the *Amplified* version: "...according to His plan..." (AMP). That phrase stuck in my mind all afternoon: "according to His plan."

Leaning over the bathtub, playing with James, I suddenly understood it. His plan. His purpose. His way. What is His way? Have faith in God. Fear not. Rejoice always. Give thanks always. Be anxious for nothing. And on and on.

The words crashed into my mind. This is His way. If you do it His way, then you can be assured that all things will work out for your good. If you have faith, rejoice, give thanks, and on and on it went.

All the scriptures I'd read welled up. And I realized that the only way I could really believe that despite the way it looked in the natural, everything was indeed going to be OK, was if I obeyed the scriptures and did it His way.

It was up to me. It was my choice. It wasn't up to Him; it was up to me. I could decide to love God and be called according to His plan and purpose, so that all things could work together for good.

This was a huge revelation. As I wrote that scripture up in large letters in my kitchen, I said, "Yes, God, I love You, and I am called according to Your plan and purpose. I will do it Your way. I will walk by faith in Your Word and not by what I am seeing or feeling or experiencing.

I will be thankful, I will rejoice, I will trust You. And I have great confidence that You are deeply concerned about us and are causing all things to work together as a plan for good, for all of us."

Then I knew deep down with absolute conviction that we were going to be OK, just like the scriptures said. That we would have the healing and prosperity He provided for us. And my heart calmed down. And faith came. And it was unshakeable.

Dear Mary,

Isn't it dreadful that I can have such wonderful revelations, and yet a few days later, I can start feeling so tired, despondent, and down?

These thoughts come into my mind: *What about me? All I do is look after everyone else. Who cares about me? Christmas is only days away, and here I am nursing Tim, nursing Christopher, looking after James 'round the clock, doing all the domestics…. No help, no friends, no family, never invited….*

But I know I must silence these thoughts; I can't afford to spiral down, down, down. So, I talk back forcefully. I force myself to say the exact opposite of what I feel. Sometimes I sing them too:

"This will be our best Christmas ever!"
"We are all strong, healthy and happy."
"I love looking after my beautiful family."
"I have formidable energy."
"I am God's princess. He adores me."
"Timothy and James are strong, healthy, and healed in every way."
"Christopher loves and appreciates me."
"Christopher is grateful for all I do."
"This will be the best Christmas yet."

Sometimes tears stream down my face because I want so much for all this to be true. And the words make me stronger, even in my emotions.

I've learned to look away from our circumstances to His plan, His way. I must trust what He said and promised and let that buoy me up with hopeful expectation.

Worrying, complaining, feeling sorry for myself because of our situation and circumstances, would be to decide to actively take the matter out of His hands, and to forgo the promise of all things working for our good.

Dear Mary,

Christmas Eve, and all is well. James has calmed down. He is playing happily and being quite cooperative. Timothy is much better and has cheered up. Even Christopher has emerged from his room, not exactly exuding energy, but he's cheerfully up and about.

Dear Mary,

Merry Christmas! We've had a lovely day. The four of us linked together with love and laughter. Filled with joy and delight as we opened our gifts. God is good, and all is well.

Of course, James has been "making friends" with his gifts for the past few weeks, not just today. I buy the toys. I tell him they are for Christmas, not for now, and put them under his bed. Periodically, he will take them out and look at them before pushing them back under the bed. On Christmas Day, he recognizes them as he pulls the wrapper off, and is delighted to be able to play with them at last.

With both the boys, we've had to do this "making friends" thing before Christmas. When Tim was younger, he'd be so overwhelmed with unexpected gifts, he'd put them away for weeks before getting used to them enough to unpack and use them. We've learned not to surprise them.

But this Christmas, Tim asked us to surprise him, and we did! It was such fun. He has changed so much and continues to get better and better!

CHAPTER 23

Dear Mary,

Psalm 27:13-14—I would have despaired had I not believed that I would see the goodness of the Lord In the land of the living. Wait for and confidently expect the Lord (AMP).

Psalm 46:1—God is our refuge and strength, a very present help in trouble.

I love the Bible. There's always something to help and encourage us. There are things in there that just go straight to the heart. Now I know I'm never having to cope on my own; He's always there, helping and encouraging me. I just have to open the Word, and He speaks to me! It's wonderful.

Christopher's better, and has thrown himself wholeheartedly back into his work. He really does give his best. I'm so grateful, and I keep praying for him, and thanking God for my lovely husband.

Tim's better too. Actually, he's simply amazing. He's recently turned 13, can you believe it? A teenager! He's changing. I suddenly notice things, little things here and there. The way he holds himself and the way he walks have changed. Things that would've stressed him out and caused a major meltdown barely faze him now. He's becoming quite pragmatic.

His joints don't seem to be giving him as much trouble as they used to. Oh, and food! Huge changes! He actually eats sandwiches now. I'm allowed to put the ham on the bread!

Remember how he wouldn't eat things if one food was touching another? Now I can put everything on one plate instead of lots of little plates, and he's getting much more adventurous.

The most amazing thing though, is how he copes with James, who's still being very difficult and tries to do whatever he can to annoy Timothy. Recently he discovered that if he creeps up behind Timothy and makes a sudden loud noise, Tim gets really upset. So, he does it whenever he can. If Tim's reading a book, he'll try to close the book or take it away. He went from not noticing Tim at all, to doing everything he can to upset him!

It's not just Tim though; he does it to me too. He wants us to get cross with him. He seems to take pleasure in our displeasure. How odd is that? I prayed about it, then Tim, Christopher, and I came up with a strategy.

We decided to "love him by faith." Whatever he does, we won't react negatively to him, no matter what. If he's pleased with our displeasure, we simply will not be displeased. So, we ignore the bad stuff and look for any opportunity to tell him he's a good boy and that we love him very much.

No matter how upset we are by his behavior, we can't show any annoyance because that's what he's after. We have to be consistent, acting pleased, completely unconcerned or bored by his antics.

Tim has taken this to heart. His patience and love for James knows no bounds. It's just not natural, especially for a boy who's had Tim's issues. But even the average 13-year-old wouldn't have anything near the patience Tim shows to James.

I know it's the Holy Spirit helping him. So, the next time James snatched Tim's book out of his hands and ran off, Tim calmly said, "What a strong boy you are, Jamie, and you can run so fast. You're a very good runner."

James responded furiously, "No! No! No! Pimmy, you thapothe be cwoth!" ("Timmy, you're supposed to be cross!") But Tim is never cross. He just takes a deep breath and finds something to praise James for. It's amazing to witness.

The other day I burnt myself in the kitchen and shouted "B----r!" at the top of my voice. James immediately started to do the same. For days afterwards, he kept on shouting that word over and over again. Tim was mortified!

I have to be more careful. James loves shouting his own made-up expletives. It sounds like he's swearing in another language, but now I've given him a real British swear word to use!

Dear Mary,

The weeks are passing, as we continue with "Operation Jamie," hunting for the slightest reason to praise him. I spend my days praying in tongues as often as possible. Oh, my goodness, do we have to dig deep for patience!

I sing little songs about how much we love James, making them up as I go along about what a lovely and good boy he is. It's quite funny in some ways, but really serious too in others.

I will never give up. I know that the Word is true. I know that autism is a defeated foe. I will not let it stay. I've made a big sign in the sitting room: AUTISM IS THE ENEMY, AND THE ENEMY HAS BEEN DEFEATED.

The other day I shouted out, "Autism is the enemy!" and James answered without looking up, "and the enemy has been defeated." He said it almost perfectly too…. So, I said, "Amen to that."

I'm praying that God will connect me with someone else to pray over the boys. Someone else who really, really believes as I do (Matt. 18:19).

I could do with some spiritual support from a person of faith. I've asked God to send me someone.

Dear Mary,

We have breakthrough! Tim and I keep laughing and thanking God. It's wonderful!

I was singing my "I love Jamie" song and talking to "the wall" about how he's such a lovely boy, and a good boy, stuff like that.

He used to answer me back, shouting, "No, no, no good boy!" But he's given up and mostly just ignores me. I talk to "the wall" all the time about what a lovely boy James is.

Today he was parking his cars in a row, and started muttering to himself, "Mamie good boy. Mamie lovely boy. Yeth, good boy, Mamie."

It was risky, but I decided to interact, so I said, "Yes darling, you are a lovely boy, and we love you very much." He looked me in the eye and said, "Yeth," smiling.

Phew, it was like the sun came out and all the angel hosts sang the hallelujah chorus right there in our sitting room!

He changed overnight. It was as if the real James was set free. Every trace of contrariness disappeared. Instead, we enjoyed a smiling little boy, eager to please. I watched as his relationship with Timothy improved. What a joy to see them connect and interact with one another. They tickled one another and wrestled on the floor playing rough.

That has never happened before. Thank You, Lord.

Now James follows Timothy around like an adoring puppy. He watches him play on the computer and X-Box. Timothy has become James's role model, the big boy he wants to become.

Every night as I clean the kitchen, I praise God while Christopher plays with the boys. Some nights tears stream down my face as I look out and see them playing together. A father with both his sons, connected and interacting with him. This is a new and mindboggling change in family dynamics, especially for James.

I spoke to the neuro-psychologist the other day. I was hoping she could assess James and do a report like she did for Timothy.

But she said she wouldn't be able to. She can usually assess patients from three years old, but even though James is five now, because of his developmental delays, his mental age is still about two-ish.

She was very keen to connect me with people regarding special therapy. I took all the names and numbers, but I have since thrown them away.

I have to laugh! God is doing the impossible, and it's ludicrous of me to think now that these people have anything to offer us.

Dear Mary,

Oh, my word! Creepy things have been going on here! When Christopher was away on a business trip recently, I was sure I heard things going on downstairs once or twice. But I dismissed it.

Then he went away again (this time for two weeks), and the noises started again. The other night after getting the boys to bed, I made sure that all doors were locked, and I turned off the television, computer, and all electronics. Then I turned off the lights and went to bed.

But I woke hours later to the sound of voices coming from downstairs. At first, I thought it was one or both of the boys. Maybe one of them had somehow sleepwalked and found himself in the lounge. So, I went and checked, and both were in bed asleep.

Looking at the clock, I realized that it was the early hours of the morning. I prayed, asking God for help and protection because I was sure that someone was in the house.

Then I crept downstairs. The sitting room light was on, and the TV was blaring.

I was freaked out, but had to look around for an intruder, an open window or door. Knowing my boys were upstairs made me braver than I really felt.

I searched the house, looking for broken glass—any explanation as to how the intruders got in, but there was nothing. I prayed while I switched everything off again and went back upstairs to lie awake in bed for a long time.

The next night I woke up at 11 p.m. to the sound of the pipes rattling, indicating that someone had switched on the faucet downstairs. I rushed down and switched them off. The lights were on again, and once more there was no sign of anyone.

This was seriously creepy. I had to admit that this was some sort of poltergeist activity, and I was terrified. I walked around downstairs, praying in all the rooms. Then I put on a praise and worship CD downstairs, left it running on loop, and went to bed.

The next day I called a number of local churches. One by one they made excuses: I wasn't a member of the church, so they couldn't come out; the pastor was leaving for his holiday; they are too busy now.

After seven phone calls, I realized that they wouldn't come. Not one of them.

As the evening settled in I became more and more anxious, but as I was putting the boys to bed, indignation rose up in me. My protective instincts came to the fore, and I became angrier and angrier.

I was furious with the pastors who didn't have the gumption to help me. I was furious that evil spirits were messing about in my house.

And I decided that enough was enough; I was not putting up with this another night!

I had noticed that all the activity only went on when I was not in the room. As long as I was there, all was quiet. So, I spoke to the Lord, "I'm trusting You to help me. I'm staying down here until someone comes to help me. I'm not going to bed until these demons are made to leave, even if I have to stay up all night.

"You'd better make one of those pastors change their minds. Wake them up, do what You have to do, but I'm not going to bed until I get help."

I settled down to wait. And no one came. I decided to pray in tongues while I waited. I knew God would help me. I assumed that He would convict someone's heart, and he would knock on my door. I was ready and waiting.

To pass the time I began flipping through the television channels, and I found an interview with Nicky Cruz. I'd read about Nicky's life in the book, *The Cross and the Switchblade*, and I'd seen the movie.

He was talking about his life before he found Jesus. He had been in a gang in New York and was full of hate and violence.

He had grown up in Puerto Rico and had a dreadful childhood, full of abuse. His mother was a witch, so séances, satanic worship, and all sorts of demonic activity were simply a normal part of his childhood.

Suddenly, he looked directly at me through the TV and said, "You don't have to put up with demonic activity in your home. I'm going to walk through your house with you right now. We're going to get rid of every demon."

God had sent Nicky Cruz to me! I leapt up, filled with righteous indignation and power. He proceeded to verbally walk me from the front door through the rest of the house. As he commanded demons to leave, so did I.

When it was done, peace reigned in our house and in my heart. I went to bed praising God for answering my prayers and sending help.

I knew He would. After that, there was no more poltergeist activity.

Dear Mary,

I'm bored, bored, bored. I'm bored with being stuck in the house year after year, doing domestic stuff all the time, and never going out. I want to eat something that someone else has cooked for a change. I want a change in this routine. A routine I seem to have been stuck in for so many years now.

Last night, I was cooking dinner and wondering how long it was since Christopher and I had been out to dinner.

It was years and years ago. I started daydreaming about us all going out to a snazzy restaurant, then I quickly shook myself and banished the thought.

Almost immediately, I heard the Lord in my heart: *"Dare to dream."*

What? I'd often stopped myself from daydreaming, thinking it was a sign of ingratitude. I wondered if I'd heard right, so I stopped what I was doing and became quiet for a moment.

"Dare to dream." I suddenly had an image of a fairy godmother saying, *"You shall go to the ball, Cinderella!"*

I laughed, and immediately I imagined all of us in a lovely restaurant, ordering off the menu—wearing nice clothes, being waited on, not worried about the expense, eating the food, laughing and chatting, leaving a big tip, because we could afford to. It was lovely!

Then I thought about the cinema. What if we could all go to the cinema together, just like a normal family?

I imagined all four of us in the car on the way to the cinema, playing music and singing along. I imagined James talking animatedly, understanding the world around him. I imagined the boys walking into the crowded room, perfectly at ease. I saw us eating popcorn happily in our seats.

I had never dared to dream like this. This is what other families did, not us. But I dared to imagine it, and as I did so, I realized that if I really believed the boys were being healed, then I could dare to dream. This was exactly what we should expect!

We had lived this quiet, isolated life for so long, could I really dare to believe we would actually have a chance of a normal life?

Well, I'd been given permission to dream. I asked the Lord to help me see in my heart what we could expect, and finally I can see us as a normal family, with normal children, and a normal life. It was wonderful.

Needless to say, dinner was late that night!

CHAPTER 23

Dear Mary,

I found a local church that believes in healing, but it was large and crowded, and as loud as a disco! There was no way the boys could come with me. And because it was so huge, I just stood around on my own.

I discovered that they had small groups, one near where we lived. So, I decided to go there instead, leaving the boys with Christopher.

I was so excited, yet nervous. People were taking turns to share, and then be prayed for. When it was my turn, I told them that our boys have a diagnosis of autism, but that God had promised to heal them. I explained that we'd already seen improvements. I expected them to be delighted and impressed, and praise God.

But the room went quiet. People looked at the carpet, they looked at the ceiling and out of the window, anywhere but at me. They were very uncomfortable. One of the women looked at me with a sad, sympathetic expression.

Then they started praying, pleading with God to help us, have mercy on us, give us strength and wisdom to raise our special boys, begging Him to heal them.

Just then my phone went. It was Christopher sending an SOS. James was awake and freaking out. I needed to get home immediately. Relieved to have an excuse to leave, I was out like a shot, and on my way home.

I said, "Lord, I know they were trying to be kind, but they didn't believe me."

"No, sweetheart," He replied, "they didn't believe Me. Stay away from unbelief."

I was so disappointed. I'd pinned my hopes on having a strong church family to support us through our healing journey. I was also hoping for some answers. There were so many things I still didn't understand.

I've been praying more fervently than ever that God would send a strong person of faith, who genuinely believes.

Timothy is making slow but steady progress, and although James has finally been showing the odd sign of improvement, we're still miles away from where we were this time last year.

He sent Nicky Cruz, so I know He'll send someone to help me and pray with me over our boys.

I need James to sleep now. I really, really need him to sleep. I pray over him every night. I pray in tongues when he's "carrying on." The other night I just lost it and started punching my pillow, screaming like a mad woman at 3 a.m. It's enough to send you stark raving mad. I just need some sleep.

The other day I was driving out of Tesco's car park and forgot which side of the road I was supposed to be on. There was a roundabout, and I couldn't remember if I should go left or right. I panicked and stalled the car. They were hooting behind me and finally started driving around me to get past. I watched where they went so I could follow them.

Then I started driving to our old house (there have been so many, it's no surprise I suppose). I remembered just in time that we had moved (more than a year ago). But my mind is going. I need some sleep.

Dear Mary,

Have you heard of Andrew Wommack? He's an American minister on TV. I usually only watch Joyce Meyer, Believer's Voice of Victory, and Creflo Dollar. I don't really like shouty American male preacher types.

But there was a video testimony of a little girl named Hannah Terradez, who was healed of a rare autoimmune disease called Eosinophilic Enteropathy. The Terradezes are a British family. When Andrew Wommack was told all about what was wrong with Hannah, he responded, "Piece of cake for Jesus."

I loved that! This man is not intimidated by how bad it looks or how incurable it is. I knew he certainly wouldn't be intimidated by autism!

We all watched the video, Timothy and I mopping our eyes, Christopher looking intrigued. In the video, Hannah's mother said something that struck me: "This guy really believes this, doesn't he?"

That was it! This is the person I've been praying for, someone to agree with me in prayer. Someone who really, really believes! Before the program was even completely finished, Christopher was on the computer in the other room looking up the ministry website. Tim and I just smiled at each other through our tears, and Tim said, "Aslan's on the move."

In less than a minute, Christopher shouted from the study, "He'll be in the UK in a few weeks!"

"You're serious? Andrew Wommack, the minister on TV?" "Yes, he's coming to a conference at his Bible school in Walsall."

"That's it! We're going!" I yelled back, dancing around the sitting room.

He returned smiling, saying, "That would be great, but…." He raised his eyebrows and looked at James.

"Yes, I know it's daunting, but we're going. It will be fine." Of course, it will be fine. I've been praying, and here is my answer! God will help us.

"Lord, we're going to need a miracle just to get us there." But then, with God, nothing is impossible, is it? God's arranging things, and He'll help us.

Dear Mary,

James had not left the house for more than nine months, and just getting him in the car would be a challenge. So, I phoned Andrew Wommack's ministry office and spoke to a lovely woman called Jane. I explained our situation and the issues we have with traveling, eating, and sleeping.

She asked, "What can you believe for?"

"What do you mean?"

"What are you expecting?"

"Well, with James starving, and none of us getting any sleep, I can believe that we'll be there for the Saturday morning service, but I'm not sure we'll be able to get them out of the car and inside the building."

"That's fine," she said. "If you can't get them out of the car, we'll send a prayer team out to you. I can't promise that it will be Andrew, but they will get prayer."

Then she prayed with me about all the concerns we have about actually getting there: the change in the routine, the different food, the different beds, all the traveling.

"We declare right now that you will make it to the meeting," she prayed. "They will eat. They will sleep!" I put the phone down and told Christopher what she'd said.

"Yeah, well, she's never met our boys, has she!"

Dear Mary,

Two weeks to go! I've explained to the boys that we're going to the meeting. Tim is thrilled, but James is very distressed. I've made a calendar for him. Every day, when we mark off another day, he cries and gets so upset.

He's slowly starting to talk, "Pease, pease, no go Mummy!" He devises all sorts of alternative plans that involve Christopher and Timothy going, while I stay home with him.

But I am adamant, and the countdown continues. I feel so sorry for him, poor little chap, he's so frightened of leaving the house, and really, really doesn't want to go. He gets into his spinning chair, pulls the hood down, and spins 'round and 'round.

All we can see are these little feet sticking out from the bottom of the chair. I tell him that God's looking after us, and we'll be OK. I pray over him that God will take away the fear, and James will be set free.

I keep singing "Friends in High Places." I love that song.

Dear Mary,

Well, we did it! We went!

It started out with James arching his back, crying, and refusing to get into the car. But I sat in the driveway, with him on my lap, and prayed, "Lord I know You are sorting this all out for us. I don't want my little Jamie to be terrified and upset. Please help him, Lord."

I remembered that we'd prayed about this already, so I knew James would be OK.

Christopher and Tim sat patiently in the car. A few minutes later, James smiled and said in a perfectly clear voice, "Mamie weddy. Leth go." We strapped him in, and he sat there, calm as a cucumber. I was praising God in my heart.

We got stuck in heavy traffic jams, making the trip much longer than we'd expected. The afternoon sun blazed into the windows, and I put a blanket up to stop it from glaring in James's eyes. He never once complained.

I read him a few stories. He was calm and cheerful. No meltdowns. No storms. Timothy didn't complain. He didn't get carsick, which was unusual. Christopher and I just stared at one another in amazement.

We went straight to our hotel, where James bounced on the bed as though it was a great adventure. Tim kept looking at me quizzically, with raised eyebrows, and I grinned back at him. Christopher just shook his head. This was all so unusual.

We decided to eat at a KFC next to the hotel; in fact, the very same restaurant that the Terradez family had been to and talked about in their story, where their daughter ate her first solid meal. If only KFC knew that their restaurant had played such an important part in these stories.

Timothy ordered himself popcorn chicken and fries. We didn't order anything for James, knowing that if we offered him food and he didn't like it, he would start heaving.

As usual, we put our food out, so he could eat anything if he wanted to. He hadn't eaten for 11 hours, and for almost a year, he'd refused all food except porridge!

He sat there looking at all the food. There were no watery eyes and heaving, which usually happened when he smelled food.

A few minutes later, James pointed at Tim's food and said, "Wath dath?"

"It's popcorn chicken, James."

"Ooohh, chik'n chik'n."

So, we handed him one of the chicken pieces, and he ate it.

Christopher and I looked at one another in shock. "Hmmm," he said when he finished eating it. "Timmy, mine!"

He took Tim's food and polished it off. When he finished it, he said, "More, more!"

Dear Mary,

We ordered more food, and he ate it all. He ate more than we'd ever seen him eat at one sitting in his life. He ate the chicken, and he ate the fries. We laughed. Aslan *was* on the move.

"It's a miracle," I said, "and we haven't even gotten there yet."

Feeling as though we had stepped into an alternative reality, we went back to our hotel, where the boys lay down in their beds and went to sleep. Christopher's eyes were wide with surprise.

I lay in bed just thanking God before falling into a deep sleep.

And then, at around midnight, we woke to a flashing red light in the ceiling. A booming, automated voice announced, "This is a fire alarm. Please make your way to the outside of the building immediately."

This repeated warning, combined with a screaming siren and a flashing light made for a horrific blast to the senses. *Oh no!* I thought, *this is going to ruin everything.*

We bundled everyone up, dragging on our coats and shoes and joining a group of people huddled on the stairs outside the building.

Twenty minutes later, we were informed that it was a false alarm, and that we could return to our rooms. Some teenage girls had had too much to drink, setting off the fire alarms with their cigarettes.

It would have been impossible to orchestrate a worse scenario for children with sensory issues.

In the past, the flashing lights, booming voice, and terrible sirens would've been enough to trigger them into a terrible state. For children sensitive to bright lights, sudden loud noises, and who became distressed at any change of the routine, nothing could've been worse.

And yet, both boys were calm and stoic and went back to bed, where James chatted for a while, suggesting suitable forms of punishment for the perpetrators of the false alarm. ("Bad peoples, the polith muth pud dem in da jaiw!") Then he fell asleep.

Christopher and I stared at one another, too surprised for words. I lay in bed thanking God for His gracious kindness. The feeling of enormous relief and gratitude was overwhelming, and the tears just poured out quietly onto my pillow.

Dear Mary,

The next morning, we went to breakfast and watched James gobble up his food. He took a dry Weetabix and munched it like a cookie!

Then we made our way to the meeting. When we arrived, James climbed out of the car without any drama. Inside, Christopher took

James to the foyer coffee shop with a basket of toys. The plan was that we'd decided to take turns, one of us listening to Andrew, the other staying with James.

The meeting was very crowded, so Timothy and I sat in the back. Tim, who'd watched Andrew on TV with me at home, was quite thrilled to see him in the flesh.

I loved listening to him, and only wished I could stay for the whole conference. However, James was getting restless. When they stopped for a tea break, people stood in line to meet Andrew, have their books signed, and ask for prayer.

I called Christopher, who brought James, and we all joined the back of the line.

Andrew had been preaching for hours, which he would do for the next several days, but he took no break, praying for people and signing books.

There were about five people in front of us when Andrew announced that the break time was over. "Will everyone please go and sit down?" he asked, turning away.

No, no, no! I thought, sudden tears streaming down my face. We are so close, we can't stop now. Not after all this. I knew that I had to do something, but I didn't know what. So, I prayed.

Lord, help me, help me, help me; I'm not going home without this man praying for my sons.

Just then, the Director of the College, Paul Flannigan, noticed my tears and how upset we all were. Without really thinking, he grabbed us and shoved us forward, saying, "Andrew, Andrew, just one more."

Andrew turned to us. You could see that he was keen to get on with the meeting, but instead he said, "OK, what can I pray for you?"

"Both boys have been diagnosed with autism," I said in a faltering voice, my heart thumping in my chest.

He put a hand on Timothy's shoulder. "Are you ready to be healed?"

"Yes!" Timothy declared. So, he put a hand on each child and prayed, rebuking autism and commanding healing.

Then he smiled at Christopher and me and said, "You are now the parents of normal, healthy children."

It was all over in less than two minutes!

CHAPTER 24

Dear Mary,

Andrew went back to the meeting, but we were all a bit stunned. Having gotten to the meeting, only then to be so close to missing out. And then for it to happen but be over so quickly. It was a very intense couple of minutes.

So, we slipped out of a side door to the car park. I wiped away my tears as we climbed into the car.

We sat there for a minute in silence. And it was James who broke the tension. "Well, that wathent tho bad."

We all burst out laughing hilariously. What better commentary could be made!

"That was quick," said Christopher, and I knew exactly what he meant. He'd taken time off work, there had been all the planning, the hotel cost and all the palaver, and we'd been in front of Andrew for such a small about of time!

"Yes," I responded, "but we are now the parents of normal healthy children!" And he smiled.

We laughed and chatted all the way to McDonald's, where James proceeded to devour another meal of chicken nuggets!

Tim was quite quiet and thoughtful. For him, nothing outwardly dramatic had happened, but for both him and me, there had been one dramatic shift.

It was no more getting healed or will be healed. From that moment on, it was done. Tim *knew* he was healed.

When we got home that afternoon, James ran across the road to the little girl who lived there. He hadn't played with her for about a year.

"Come play!" he called. Christopher, Tim, and I watched as they played in the sandpit, ran around the lawn, and jumped on the trampoline. They played together for the rest of the afternoon. Little Khloe smiled at me sweetly. "I missed Jamie," she said. "I'm glad he's back."

Yes, he's back! Our precious boy is free. I watched his happy little face as he charged about, talking and laughing with his friend. Oh God, thank You so much.

Christopher kept shaking his head, saying, "Wow, is this our little Jamie? I can't believe my eyes!"

"We knew it, didn't we, Mother dear?" Timothy smiled at me, "We knew. We just knew."

"Yes, darling," I laughed, hugging him. "Because if it says so... then it is so," he finished with a grin.

Lord, I know You have a good future for Tim. Help him to walk that path. He's missed out on so much, make it up to him, Lord, please.

My little prayer partner, my son, who knows how to believe God. He'd had no doubts whatsoever that he and James were destined to be healed.

That night, James had the first complete, unbroken, peaceful night's sleep that he'd had since the day he was born. I lay next to him, waking up and looking at him on and off all night, his angelic little face resting on his pillow.

All those nights of rage, fear, and distress. Now he has peace. It's miraculous! Thank You, Lord.

Dear Mary,

I am the mother of normal, healthy children. I've been saying that over and over again. Andrew may have spoken those words, but it was Jesus who spoke them to me. That statement is burned onto my mind and heart forever.

Jesus said, *"It is finished,"* when He hung on the cross (John 19:30).

It is finished. Well, that's what's happened here. It is done. The boys are healed. That's it. Done. Sorted. We are now the parents of normal healthy children. Thank You, Lord.

Dear Mary,

Any lingering symptoms or characteristics will now just fall away because they are healed. They are healed, and I'm so happy, so relieved.

A few days after Andrew prayed for him, James woke up in the night heaving and threw up. After I'd settled him again, I wondered if perhaps his body was still just getting used to solid food.

But it happened again the next night. By the third night, I knew we had a problem. I remembered what Ashley Terradez had done when his daughter Hannah had started heaving in a very similar way. He took his authority and spoke to the symptoms, commanding them away.

So I spoke to James's body: "I command nausea and vomiting to go. You are to accept and digest food properly in Jesus' name!"

And the vomiting stopped. It's so funny, only a few weeks ago I asked James when he would sleep in his own room, and he had put up three little fingers and said, "When I forty." Praise God, two weeks after Andrew prayed for him, we moved him into his own room, where he has been happily ensconced ever since!

No tears, no aggression, no night terrors, nothing. Just smiles and peace. "Gooda nighta, Timmy. Gooda nighta, Daddy. Gooda nighta, Mummy. Thee you mordin." (See you in the morning.) What a joy. My little blessing.

He's eating well and is even joining us at the table now. After meals, he lifts up his shirt to be complemented on his tummy! We all have to exclaim how beautiful and big it is, what a big boy he is, etc., while he wriggles and giggles and pats his little tummy in delight.

"Pees, tankoo, you're weltom…." He's becoming so polite!

It's like he's woken up and is slowly starting to notice the world around him.

He started dressing himself, pajamas for indoors and clothes for outdoors. After a while he stopped bothering to change back into his pajamas when he came in.

And that was it. So many firsts, just unfolding naturally. Initially, he'd only wear the same trousers and shirt every day.

"Mummy," he said one day, "Callum (another new friend he now has) wears different clothes every day."

"Yes, darling, most people do." The next morning, I walked into his room and found shirts spread all over his floor as he debated which one to wear. He'd not only noticed that Callum existed, he'd even noticed what he wore from day to day.

He had one odd habit that hadn't stopped. He hoarded his outgrown clothes and socks, refusing to get rid of them. He hid them in a bundle at the back of a drawer in the hope that I wouldn't find them. In the past, when I'd tried taking them, he'd become so distressed that I just left them there.

One day, I found him laughing in his room. "Why am I keeping all these old things?" he asked.

"I've no idea, darling. It would be good to give them to the thrift shop, so a smaller boy could wear them." That was a risky thing to say. In the past, the idea of anyone else having his things would have enraged him.

"Yes," he said, looking at the bundle of clothes in his arms, "I think you're right." He handed me the bundle and heaved a deep sigh of relief. "Ahh, that's better," he said.

He had the same issue with toys. He'd be furious at the mere suggestion of giving any away. I used to hide his old toys for six months. If he didn't notice they were gone, I'd get rid of them. Most of the time, he'd hang onto toys long after he'd outgrown them.

"James, would you like to sort through your toys with me?" I asked, feeling hopeful.

He agreed. "I don't need this anymore," he said tossing his old toys in a pile. "We can give this away… and this. Really, I'm a big boy now, and I don't need all this little boy stuff."

He even came across of box of Bob the Builder figures and vehicles that he'd adored but made a dismissive wave of his hand and dispensed with them.

His reaction to cleaning out toys was so extreme, that I felt a little nervous about getting rid of them. Instead, I hid them in the garage for a few weeks.

One day I said, "Oh look, James, here's all the stuff you threw out. Shall we take it to the thrift shop now?"

He picked up a toy with a wistful expression and said, "Oh, I used to love this." Then he dropped it and walked off. "You do it, Mummy."

And that was that. He never squirreled away his belongings, hoarding things he didn't need anymore. No drama. No fuss.

Dear Mary,

About this time, I noticed that he'd started smelling of body odor. I thought it a bit early for this to be happening as he was still only six. I also realized that it wasn't just body odor, but facial hair had appeared on his top lip, and acne marred his smooth baby skin.

He'd started premature adolescence. Christopher and I were appalled.

Tim had started adolescence at nine, which I thought then was early. But this was ridiculous.

I waited until he was asleep, then went to his bedside and gently touched his back: "I command adolescence to go away," I said. "Don't come back until he's eleven."

His skin cleared up, the body odor went away, and his facial hair fell out.

Dear Mary,

I'm so grateful for Andrew Wommack's book *The Believer's Authority*. I'm finding that I have plenty of opportunities to use my authority!

I looked at James in the bath one night recently and noticed little red dots all over his body.

Now that he'd become sociable and playing with other children, he'd caught chicken pox. There were a few little red spots on his skin, which I knew would turn into blisters.

It's just a mild case, and then he'll be immune, I thought, applying a little calamine lotion before putting him to bed.

The next morning, he was so covered with red spots that I could barely see a clear patch of skin. The child had the worst case of chicken pox I'd ever seen. Concerned about his immunity, I'd not thought to resist the disease. I knew that every one of those spots would soon be blisters unless I did something right now.

"I command every one of those spots to leave him in Jesus' name!" I said. "Blisters, I command you to scab over and heal immediately!"

By the next morning, the red dots had disappeared. The blisters had turned to scabs. That evening at bath time, the scabs were falling off, and his skin was healing. I'd learned my lesson.

When the little girl across the street came down with conjunctivitis (Pink Eye), I offered to look after her so that her mother could go to work.

James loves her coming 'round because they have such fun playing together. Afterwards, every time she was ill, she stayed with us. Her mother soon realized that I wasn't worried about James or anyone in our family catching anything, because I prayed, and they never did.

The child came down with the flu, coughs, colds, and all the typical childhood diseases. If anyone in my family got a single symptom, I commanded the symptoms to leave. Then I prayed healing scriptures over us. Those symptoms couldn't stay.

One day, James's friend was sent home from school really ill, having caught Bird Flu! She had a high fever, and her mother was anxious. We soon had her cuddled up under her favorite blanket on our sofa.

As her mum was leaving, she thanked me profusely, and said, "You work your special magic on her!"

I said, "Yes, I'll pray." James and I held her hands and commanded sickness to go, then she and James settled down to watch a DVD. By afternoon, the fever was gone, and the children were running around the house playing with boundless energy. Her mother was astounded when she came to pick her up later.

Dear Mary,

Another first! We did it! Just like I dreamed! We went to the cinema, all four of us together. Tim was DJ in the car, and we had a wonderful music session on the way there.

We went to see *The Voyage of the Dawn Treader.* Having read all the Narnia books to my boys many times over, they were so excited to see the movie. James proudly clutched his 3D glasses, while munching on great handfuls of popcorn.

It was just as I'd imagined! How can I ever thank God enough? There are no words to describe that experience. It was one of the many moments in our miraculous journey that I'll never forget. And Jesus was right there with us, smiling.

CHAPTER 25

Dear Mary,

I've had an interesting morning. I woke up early, as usual, to spend time reading and praying before everyone else gets up.

I was reading Romans 4:17-21, making it personal, putting my name in there, and relating it to our situation.

I do that every day at the moment, starting with, "I am Debbylee, the mother of normal healthy boys." As I was launching into Romans, I heard in my heart, *"Who? Who is Debbylee?"*

I immediately answered, "The mother of normal, healthy children!"

"Really?" Well, that perplexed me. After prayerfully thinking about it awhile, I realized that He was not questioning my belief in the boys being healed. He was questioning my belief in my own identity.

Did I really identify as the mother of healed children? And I began to realize that no, actually, without realizing it consciously, I didn't.

You see, my whole identity was wrapped up in being a fulltime caregiver. I had no identity outside of that: Chief caregiver. It's not the same as a mother of healthy children.

I had to change the way I saw myself; my whole identity had to alter, because it was based on who I was (as the mother of children with special needs) rather than who I am now.

I didn't know how to be anything else. My identity as an individual had disappeared. My entire personality had been submerged and overshadowed by the needs of my family.

I was a full-time caregiver, cook, cleaner, teacher, mother, wife, nurse. I had no personal likes or dislikes; I liked what they liked, and disliked anything that upset them.

The Lord was showing me that because that was my identity, that was how I was still relating to the boys, and I was holding them back because of it. My personal identity had to change!

Oh, my goodness! I don't want to be the one holding my children back because I don't know how else to relate to them! What an awful thought, and it hadn't even dawned on me before.

"Well, I don't know, Lord, I haven't a clue who I am. You'll have to show me."

"You are Deborah," He said. *"And she is the mother of normal, healthy children. Debbylee is history. I will show you who you are, who we are together."*

In setting my boys free to be whom He created them to be, He was setting me free too! Then I remembered the words He had spoken to me in November 2007:

The promises I put in you,
I will bring them to pass.
I will bring about restoration.
I will bring about healing.
I will restore the lost years.
If you dig your heels in,
If you refuse to give up,
I will fight the fight for you.
   Keep your eyes on the vision.
Keep your eyes on what I have promised, and you will see it happen.

Wow. I was amazed and grateful. And this is the next step—my new identity—as a healthy mother of healthy children.

I could hear that Christopher was awake, and I rushed downstairs. "Sweetheart, I'm Deborah now. I'm not Debbylee anymore; she's history. I'm Deborah now."

He stared at me for a few moments, then said, "Right, O-Kay! Shall we have a coffee?"

Over coffee, I told him what had happened. "That's great, Gertrude," he said. "I mean Phedelia. I mean… who are you again?"

Dear Mary,

And so, I've changed my name officially. On my passport, with my bank and other official documents. Debbylee's history; she is no longer needed.

I realize that, as long as I co-operate with Him, He's not only healing the boys, but our whole family dynamics. I can't trust habit, or instinct, or inclination automatically. I need to be intentionally guided by the Holy Spirit and the Word. Sensitive to and subject to His guidance. Please keep me from putting a spanner in the works, Lord!

Dear Mary,

The other night I had a dream. Jesus was telling me to stop worrying about something we'd been dealing with.

Anyway, the next day, I was in the park, pushing James on the swings, when I remembered the dream.

"Lord, You had Andrew's face in the dream. Why?" He replied, *"All those things that you've been confused about, listen to Andrew, and I'll teach you."*

I'd been learning so much from Kenneth Copeland Ministries, Joyce Meyer, and Creflo Dollar, but I knew the Lord was telling me to focus on Andrew's teachings now.

Even though things were really tight financially, we ordered all of Andrew's books and lots of other materials. I read them all: *Spirit, Soul and Body, A Better Way to Pray, You've Already Got It,* and *The Believer's Authority.*

In *The Believer's Authority,* Andrew tells an anecdote about when his little son was ill with croup. His mother eventually said, "Admit it, Andy, he's sick."

Andrew said, "I got right down there, stuck my finger in her face, and said, 'Satan, in the name of Jesus, I command you to shut up! I will not receive any of your criticism or any of your curses. My son is blessed and not cursed!'" And his son was healed.

If only I'd read this before. Instead, I'd been too "polite," and James had suffered a regression that had cost him a whole year of his life.

Dear Mary,

I haven't spoken about Timothy for a while. Well, he hasn't had any regressions, he has simply improved slowly, sometimes making great strides, and then little steps, but always getting better.

Although the "school" he attended for about 18 months hadn't offered a great deal of scholastic challenge, the staff and environment had been supportive and encouraging. He had flourished there.

An Outward Bound trip inspired his growing desire for independence and adventure. They spent a week in the country doing all sorts of team- and character-building activities and challenges. It was his first time away from home, family, and routine, and he'd had a wonderful time—what a testament to God's power.

However, he got to the point where he became more aware of the children around him, and their obvious behavioral and emotional problems.

A few months after Andrew had prayed for him, Timothy decided to leave. "I'm not like the other kids; they all have issues and I don't now, and I'm not enjoying being there anymore. I'd rather stay home," he said. He was now 13 years old.

Dear Mary,

Well time certainly is flying. It's January 2010, and we just celebrated Timothy's 14th birthday, going out for pizza. He's as tall as his father now, and his father is 6 feet 2 inches!

Andrew Wommack Ministries held another conference in Stoneleigh Park, near Coventry in the spring.

Timothy absolutely loved attending every meeting at the Youth Zone, learning so much. He's made new friends and received the gift of tongues.

He stood up in front of hundreds of kids to give his testimony, declaring, "I'm a miracle! God has healed me of Asperger's Syndrome."

The young people listened as he told his story. For Tim, this was a dream come true, to be one of the crowd, to join others in learning about and worshiping God.

It was one of the happiest times of his life. Those meetings set a foundation for him and were his first experience of being in the family of God.

The symptoms and issues Tim had have fallen away one by one, and he's now free to start growing and developing into the person God made him to be.

Christopher and I have watched him emerge from the shadows of despair to become a happy young man. He has such a great sense of humor, and is such a fun, clever, gentle, and caring boy.

Christopher says to anyone who will listen that Timothy is the funniest person he knows. The anxiety, frustration, confusion, and despair that he lived with for so long are history now.

Instead, he relishes every opportunity to be independent and adventurous, ever watchful to gain skills to cope and function in this new world he's now a part of.

Dear Mary,

One day, Tim's going to go to Charis Bible College! I know this for sure, and I am thrilled!

I picked up a *Gospel Truth* magazine the other day. There was a graduation photo of some students, and as I looked at it, I "saw" Timothy there in cap and gown.

Phew, that was really encouraging. Timothy has had so little education, and he still struggles to write. Then there's the money. We're still paying off loans and have a big mortgage, so I don't know how we'll afford it. But I know God has good plans for my boys.

I speak Jeremiah 29:11 over them regularly: "For I know the thoughts that I think toward you, says the LORD, thoughts of peace and not of evil, to give you a future and a hope"; as well as Isaiah 54:13—"All your children shall be taught by the LORD, and great shall be the peace of your children."

I'm trusting completely in Him, and I'm so grateful for these promises. Without them, we'd be in big trouble! To say our children aren't getting a normal upbringing or a normal education would be an understatement!

I know that without God we'd be stuffed!

Dear Mary,

The other day Tim decided he wanted to catch the train to Cambridge, which is about an hour away, to visit a friend there.

I can't begin to tell you how I felt, standing on Peterborough station platform, watching him board that train, turn and wave to James and me, an anxious but smiling expression on his beautiful face.

I was so nervous for him, my stomach was fluttering, and my heart was hammering away. But I was deeply grateful and excited to see him exercise his new-found freedom and independence. And, of course I prayed in tongues all day, trusting God to look after him.

Dear Mary,

After that, Timothy has made regular trips on his own.

Christopher and I are watching in awe, wonder, and unutterable delight, as he changes and flourishes before our astonished and delighted eyes.

Christopher was laughing over his coffee the other morning. "He catches trains to see his buddy in Cambridge. They go out to lunch together. He's handling money, ordering things, eating new foods. He's meeting new people, socializing. Deb, I wouldn't have thought it possible, but it's happening!"

Yes, it's happening. Timothy is free to be the real person who was there all along. Free from the evil tentacles of autism. Thank You, Lord!

Dear Mary,

Timothy came to talk to me the other day. He said, "Mother dear, I know I'm completely well now. It's time to have the autism diagnosis overturned; we need to make an appointment with the doctor."

So, I have scheduled an appointment for April 27, 2011.

Dear Mary,

What a day! What a day, Mary. Head held high, shoulders back, Tim strode into the new Peterborough Hospital, confident that his diagnosis would be removed.

"Hi, I'm Timothy," he greeted the doctor holding out his hand, smiling.

Although only 15, Tim is 6'3", broad shouldered, and handsome. The doctor looked surprised. "So, this is Tim?" he smiled, looking at me with raised eyebrows, somewhat puzzled. "I've never been asked to remove a diagnosis before, Mrs. McDermott." He asked a few questions, looking searchingly first at me, then at Tim. "So, Tim, tell me..."

Reading softly to James in the corner, I watched as they talked, the doctor taking notes. They laughed and chatted, then the doctor stood up, put out his hand to shake Tim's, and said, "Good to meet you, Tim." Then turning to shake hands with me, he laughed, saying, "There'll be no problems. There's absolutely nothing wrong with this young man. I'll be delighted to remove the diagnosis!"

Dear Mary,

A week later, in a report dated May 4, 2011, the same doctor wrote: "Timothy does not meet the criteria for the diagnosis of Asperger's Syndrome at this time. He does not have significant qualitative difference in communication, social interaction, and repetitive and stereotyped activity that significantly interferes with his function.

"Timothy is a neurodevelopmentally typical young man, and the label of Asperger's Syndrome is not applicable. He has been discharged from my care."

When the letter arrived, I ripped it open, then shouted to Tim, "It's official, darling! You are not special anymore. You are just typical!"

We laughed and hugged, dancing around the sitting room, Tim punching the air, shouting "RESULT!" James joined in, dancing and laughing and whooping.

That evening, as Christopher's car drew up in the drive, Tim flew out with the letter, waving it about and thrusting it under Christopher's nose.

My heart melted, as I watched father and son hugging in the driveway. Christopher looked over Tim's shoulder at me, tears in his eyes, "That's good news big son, that's very, very good news!" Christopher was the happiest father on earth!

Of course, I was delighted too Mary. It was great to have it made official.

However, I did my real celebrating on Mother's Day, four years ago.

What a journey we've all been on.

Dear Mary,

So, we moved to Walsall towards the end of last year (I think this is move number 13, but I can't be sure). All sorts of things went wrong, but God is good, and all is now well!

We've been happily ensconced here for about eight months.

Its spring 2012, James is eight now, and getting on really well.

The other day we were driving down the motorway, and I heard James trying to say something. "Thay, thain, thains...." It was a Sainsbury's delivery truck, and he was trying to read the words on its side.

I knew immediately, this is the time to start teaching him reading, writing, and math. What a different experience it is from trying to teach a child with learning difficulties! What a joy. He's such a conscientious little fellow.

Christopher and I have been chatting: Apart from a slight speech impediment, he seems absolutely fine to us now. The local doctor referred us to the autism team at Midlands Psychology Unit. "I'd like the diagnosis of autism removed," I told the doctor.

"Mrs. McDermott," she replied smiling at me, "even children with autism progress and improve. I'm really glad your son is improving, but it doesn't mean he doesn't have autism."

"I've read his notes, but where are all his assessments for the past five years?" she asked, looking through his medical records.

"I stopped taking him to be assessed when he was three," I replied.

She looked surprised. "Well, let's have a chat with James...."

Delighted with his attentive audience, James launched into details about the latest Chip, Biff and Kipper book he was reading.

He told her all about how he and Tim loved ice skating. All the while happily working out the various activities she wanted him to do.

She asked a speech and language therapist and an occupational therapist to do an assessment. I just sat there smiling. I could almost feel Jesus sitting there with me, leaning back, arms folded, and occasionally winking at me!

Finally, she sat back, shrugged, and said, "This child and these records do not match. There is nothing wrong with James. This diagnosis is a mistake and must be removed from his records immediately!"

And so, it was.

Dear Mary,

I am Deborah, the mother of normal healthy boys. The octopus of autism is dead. Every malignant tentacle withered away.

When I discovered that Jesus had paid for our healing 2000 years ago, I realized that God didn't have to do anything. It was up to us to receive what He had already provided. When I stopped cooperating with the enemy through believing, fearing, and speaking autism, it was starved of any power to stay. It's up to me, to us, to believe and receive what has already been accomplished. Thank You, Lord, for Your Word, Your Holy Spirit, and Your people, who have taught me and helped us on this journey.

And dear Mary, after all that we have been through together, all the despair and hopelessness and all the joy and laughter, now our boys are free to be who God created them to be.

I have a final question for you: Do you believe in miracles?

THE END.

Cambridgeshire and Peterborough
NHS Foundation Trust

Please reply to:
Child Health Department
City Care Centre
1st Floor Admin Area B
Thorpe Road
Peterborough PE3 6DB

Our Ref:
Your Ref:
Date: 4th May 2011

Tel: 01733 776388
Fax: 01733 776354
Website: www.cpft.nhs.uk

CONFIDENTIAL – MEDICAL REPORT

Name: Timothy McDermott **D.O.B:**

Address: **GP:**

School: HOME TUITION **NHS No:**

Date Seen: 27th April 2011

Reason for Consultation: To review whether diagnosis of Asperger syndrome is an appropriate label for Timothy.

Conclusion: Timothy does not meet any criteria for the diagnosis of Asperger syndrome at the moment. He does not have significant qualitative difference in communication, social interaction and repetitive and stereotyped activities that significantly interfere with his functioning.

Plan: Timothy is a neurodevelopmentally typical young man, and the label of Asperger syndrome is not applicable. He has been discharged from my care.

I met with Timothy, his mother and his little brother in my clinic today. I looked through his notes to review all the information that is available.

INFORMATION REVIEWED

1. **The original clinic letter from Dr** **dated 1st September 2005.**
   This letter talks about difficulties with literal use of language, suboptimal eye contact and sensory sensitivities. The conclusion was that Timothy would fall within the Autism Spectrum Disorder, and a label of Asperger syndrome was proposed.

HQ Elizabeth House, Fulbourn Hospital, Cambridge CB21 5EF
T 01223 726789 F 01480 398501 www.cpft.nhs.uk

A member of Cambridge University Health Partners

MIDLANDS PSYCHOLOGY

Midlands Psychology CIC
Midland House
Stowe Court
Stowe Street
LICHFIELD
WS13 6AQ

Tel:

Our Ref:

25 May 2012

PRIVATE & CONFIDENTIAL
Mr and Mrs McDermott

Dear Mr and Mrs McDermott

Re: James McDermott – DOB:

It was good to meet you Debbylee and James at our appointment on 9 May 2012. You had asked for this appointment in order to review the diagnosis that James had been given of Autism Spectrum Disorder aged approximately 2½ when the family were living in Peterborough. This diagnosis followed some delays in James' development, particularly in his speech and language and also some identified sensory issues. During our appointment you expressed that as parents and as a family you no longer feel that this diagnosis is appropriate for James and as a result had asked if it could be removed. As a result the majority of our appointment was spent exploring traits and characteristics associated with the triad of impairment in autism to see whether these still apply to James. The following is a summary of that discussion.

Background Information

James lives at home with you, Debbylee, and your husband Christopher and his older brother Tim who is 16. Previously Tim also had a diagnosis of Asperger Syndrome which has subsequently been removed from him. Both boys are home educated by yourself and with additional support in maths via a kumon tutor.

Language and Communication

You reported that James initially had some speech delay and did not talk until he was around 4 years of age. As a much younger child James was also reported to display evidence of some echolalia and to occasionally make babbling or screeching noises in an unusual pitch. Currently, James remains having a lisp although he is relatively easy to understand in conversation and during our appointment I was able to have a number of interactions with him that were reciprocal in nature.

Social Interaction

Once again, as a much younger child, James was reported to have significant difficulties in socialising in groups of more that two people. In particular, social interactions would frequently deteriorate into fights or distress for James. From your report this appears to have significantly improved over time, James is now cooperative in his play he is adaptable with other young people and is able to go up to groups of children he does not know and

Email: enquiries@midlandspsychology.co.uk www.midlandspsychology.co.uk
Company Registration No: 06701716.

make friends. During my conversation with James, during our appointment, I had a sense of him being able to initiate friendships and having some sense of how to repair friendships when these go wrong.

Social Imagination and a Flexibility of Thought

When James was a younger child, he was reported to have a clear need for routines and that family life needed to be arranged around the routines of him and his elder brother. At this point, he also needed time to get used to anything new including in his eating and food, and at that point he had a very restricted range and diet. In addition, he had a number of particular interests as a younger child such as; trains and guns and weapons. These did appear to be repetitive and fairly inflexible in nature however over time, once again, these appear to have improved. For example; James now displays more imaginative play (this was observed in clinic), he is reported to like dressing up and role play games, and is much less fussy about food than he used to be. He is also reported to have improved commonsense, for example; to be able to be trusted to go off on his bike and meet friends on his own in the village where the family live. James was also described by yourself, Debbylee, as being good with spontaneity, in deed there was a sense that in the family this was a very important concept and part of the home education that you have for James and his brother Tim is to enable you to be able to take advantage of doing certain activities when the family feels like doing them. The fact that James responds to this spontaneity and does not require rigid routines also suggests that things have progressed and improved over time.

Sensory Issues

Previously James was reported to have a number of sensory sensitivities. He would gag and vomit if people sat too close to him or in public toilets, showed some photophobia, and some tactile sensitivity. In addition, James appeared to have some hyposensitivity to pain frequently appearing not to feel the pain of his own physical injuries. Once again, according to parental report, these appear to have dissipated over time.

Summary

As a result of our discussions and my interactions and observation with James during our appointment it is clear there has been significant progress over time in all areas associated with the triad of impairment with autism. **As a result, the label Autism Spectrum Disorder is no longer appropriate for James and should be removed from any documentation in the future that relates to him.** In order to inform the family's decision around whether James will eventually be able to start more formal schooling I offered the family the chance to have some additional speech and language therapy assessment or some additional cognitive assessment to help them think through those choices. During our appointment, Debbylee, you advised that you did not think this was necessary and as a result I will now be discharging James from our service. If, in the future, you would like any further help from our service please do not hesitate to contact us on the telephone number above.

Yours sincerely

Clinical Psychologist
Midlands Psychology CIC

c.c.

Timothy, James, Deborah and Christopher
January 2019

Made in the
USA
Monee, IL